C0-DBO-725

COST CONTROL IN BUSINESS

The Dun & Bradstreet
Business Library

New York

Thomas Y. Crowell Company
Established 1834

L.C. Card 67-2275
ISBN 0-690-21862-1

1 2 3 4 5 6 7 8 9 10

Contents

Foreword

If one factor is constant in our ever-changing business world, it is the all-consuming interest in cost control. What happens year in and year out is that after an outstanding sales job, management is often disappointed in the year-end profit picture. There is a solution: better planning and tighter control of costs.

Cost control requires careful record keeping, budgeting and analysis. The name for this job is financial management. It is a task that faces the head of the largest corporation and the owner of the smallest neighborhood business.

This book deals with the techniques of increasing profit —the keeping of records and their analysis, and the translation of this information into action. You'll find in it a case history and practical suggestions, an explanation of ratios, convenient charts on which you record your own progress and a cost control check list. These are designed to help you keep your operations moving the right way— towards greater profits for your business.

CHAPTER 1

Managing for Profit

You are in business to earn a profit. This goal is the sole reason for your expenditure of time, money and energy. Yet, surprisingly few businessmen understand what profit is, where it comes from and how to stop it from leaking away.

If you could operate your business on a strictly cash basis, you might have no trouble finding out if you were making a profit. You'd receive cash for everything bought from you, and pay cash for your purchases, your payroll and all other expenses. You'd count the till every morning and again at night. If you had more money in the evening than in the morning, your business would have been profitable.

Unfortunately, very few retailers and certainly no wholesalers or manufacturers are able to operate on a strictly cash basis. Taxes, credit, financing all demand paperwork. The answer is to know your business from A to Z, so that you can quickly spot a financial problem and act to cure the ill. The wide-awake businessman continually measures and controls his business activity. This alert management of finances permits him to take advantage of every opportunity to grow and prosper.

It is as simple as this: Good salesmanship will increase your income, but only good management can increase profit.

WHAT IS PROFIT?

Profit is the key word for every businessman. Profit permits you to grow. Profit provides you and your family with the good things in life. Profit regulates the time you must devote to your business and the leisure you are able to enjoy.

Profit comes in two varieties—gross profit and net profit. Gross profit is the money you receive for your products or services minus what you pay for your raw materials or finished merchandise. Gross profit is important because it tells you how fast and far your business is progressing.

Net profit is even more important because it is your real take home pay. Net profit controls the future growth of your business. It is found by deducting all your operating expenses, including your salary, from gross profit.

It is in the area of net profit that leaks will drain away vital dollars and cents. Many businessmen never really know where these leaks are, but the wise businessman finds them quickly and acts to stop the drain on his dollars.

Earlier we said salesmanship will increase income, but only management will increase profits. What has been the trend in your company?

What were gross sales_____and net profits_____ five years ago?

What were gross sales_____ and net profit_____
last year? Then, divide gross sales into net profit for each
year and see if you are doing better or worse percentage-
wise.

5 years ago   *last year*
gross sales) net profit   gross sales) net profit

THREE TYPES OF LEAKS

To understand how profits can be drained away from
your business, you must know how much each product
or service contributes to the over-all profitability of your
business. You must learn how variations in payroll, utilities and raw materials affect your income. A broken tool,
needless absences, too big a staff—each could cost you
unnecessary dollars.

There are three major ways that net profits may be lost:

1. Errors in Managerial Judgment—Men and women
who run businesses are only human and, as a result, make
mistakes in judgment. One may overstock merchandise
that doesn't move, while another fails to have what the
public is buying. Another may let his desires for self-
gratification move him into quarters in which the over-
head will strangle him. Failure to obtain the necessary information before entering a new market or product area
is yet another possible error in judgment.

We know mistakes will be made in business. The pros-
perous businessman, however, does not make the same
mistake twice. He finds out where he went wrong and
learns from his error.

2. Careless Cost Control—Both mechanical failures and human failings waste dollars. A machine may continually ruin raw material, or a leaking valve permit fuel to drain away. There may be employee and customer dishonesty, or a failure to check the cash registers after each shift. Unless you know what your return should be, based on stock depletion, you are in trouble. The answer is to keep constant and correct records.

3. Complacency—Too often businessmen end up working for their business rather than having the business make a profit for them. The reason? They become complacent and content to run the business for a salary. This can happen to you if you fail to drive your business to its fullest potential.

To achieve the utmost success, you must be continually aware of changing market potential and ready to take advantage of new opportunities.

Can you list one business organization you know that has lost ground or even failed because of each of the errors listed above?
Errors in Managerial Judgment.................................
Careless Cost Control..
Complacency ....

The case history that follows in Chapter 2 will offer practical suggestions for businessmen who want to realize the fullest potential of their business. Our case history is about a retailer, but any wholesaler or manufacturer could easily slip himself into Bill Brady's shoes.

CHAPTER 2

Managing versus Just Operating

There are rugged individualists who feel they can fly by the seat of their pants, or literally manage by ear alone. They are, however, becoming a vanishing breed in today's complex business world. A modern businessman must know more than just where he has been, where he now stands and where he is going. He must know how to get there.

Fortunately, there are many consultants available to help businessmen grow and prosper. Some are members of a business organization's own staff. Others are for hire. In this case history we will see just how retailer Bill Brady was shown the real road to success.

"Listen, Jack," said Bill Brady to his new accountant, Jack Larkin; "selling is what counts in business."

"It certainly does, Bill," Larkin said, "but what about profits? You can't grow without profits."

"Get sales and get the right price and the profits come naturally," Brady emphasized.

"Unless your costs run away with profits. You have to keep track of where your income is going," Larkin argued.

"Cost controls in my business are a waste of time and money," Bill insisted. "I manage my business by ear. And my business shows a profit every year."

Larkin shook his head, "Of course you can't make a profit without a sale. But your profit would be higher if your costs were in line. I'll prove it to you."

Bill Brady and his wife, Mary, were partners in Brady's, a store selling dry goods and general merchandise in a small town in northern Wisconsin. Sales in Bill's business had been increasing and Bill intended to expand even further. But he wanted to be sure he was on solid ground. He had turned over to Jack Larkin the store's figures for the past year and asked Jack to "take over the books and advise me."

"In selling you're tops," continued Larkin, "but your take from the business isn't so good as it might be. You were telling me the other day you wanted to add a line of men's and women's casual clothes. What are you going to use to finance the new merchandise, to build the new shelves?"

"New shelves?" Bill exclaimed. "Why I'm thinking of building a new alcove. That window over there is coming out. The landlord has enough footage to his lot line for me to construct a nice alcove."

"How are you going to finance the construction? It's going to cost you a lot of money."

"I figure $4,500 with fixtures."

"How are you going to get the money?"

"The bank. You know my credit is good. I've had a loan at the bank every year since the store began. I always pay back promptly."

"Plus interest."

"Right. Interest is part of my monthly costs. For a while I'll have two loans to pay."

"I don't doubt the bank will help you out again. But do you realize, Bill, you might have been able to avoid interest charges and finance the expansion out of earnings?"

"Where have I gone wrong, Jack?"

"With the additional sales you are pulling in, you should be piling up bigger profits, but apparently you're not. Some of your profits are getting away through holes in your cost management policy. Tell you what, I'll analyze your costs and financial condition from the figures you and your wife gave me for your income tax returns. I'll also jot down typical operating ratios and a few typical financial ratios on dry goods and general merchandise stores. Then we can compare your results with others in your line. Let's make a date for next Wednesday, OK?"

SALES UP—PROFIT DOWN

The next Wednesday Jack Larkin returned with his analysis of Brady's operations for the year ending December 31. Here's the income statement he showed to his client, Bill Brady:

				Operating Ratios of Brady's	Typical Operating Ratios for the Line*
Net Sales:			$187,770	100%	100%
Inventory Jan. 1, 196–		$ 30,601			
Purchases	$122,698				
Less Purchase Disc.	766				
	121,932	121,932			
		152,533			
Less Inventory, Dec. 31, 196–		26,540			
Cost of Goods Sold		125,993	125,993	67.1%	70.8%
Gross Margin			61,777	32.9%	29.2%
Partners' Compensation			10,149	↓ 5.4%	7.9%
Employees' Wages			19,838	↑ 10.5%	9.6%
Occupancy Expense			8,358	↑ 4.5%	3.7%
Advertising			4,910	↑ 2.6%	1.3%
Bad Debt Losses			3,193	↑ 1.7%	0.2%
Buying Expense			2,751	↑ 1.5%	0.3%
Depreciation, Fixtures			1,379	↑ 1.0%	0.7%
All Other Expenses			9,388	↑ 5.0%	3.4%
Total Expense			60,466	↑ 32.2%	27.1%
Net Profit Before Income Tax			1,311	↓ 0.7%	2.1%
Gross Margin			61,777	32.9%	29.2%
Inventory Turnover				4.4 times	2.6 times

Based on performance of stores grouped by credit policy with credit sales 25% or more of total sales.

Jack started his analysis, "Not too much we can do about sales. They're already moving in the right direction. But we do need to take a good, hard look at expenses. In your business, it seems to me, there are two ways to build profits.

You can continue to increase sales while you hold merchandise costs and expenses in line, or you can hold sales and gross profit margins about even while you reduce expenses. There are other ways to boost profits but they don't apply to your case at the moment. As I look at your income statement I see you get a good sales volume."

"We tried for $160,000 this year and hit $187,770, thanks to our expanded credit accounts."

"Next, comparing your gross margin with that of a typical store in your line, I see yours was 32.9% or 3.7% better than the 29.2% typical gross margin. Your buying and pricing is right and apparently you keep mark-downs well under control."

"What do those arrows mean in front of the ratios for my store, Jack?"

"I put them there to emphasize where your costs are higher or lower than usual for your line. Your expenses ran 32.2% of net sales, 5.1% more than the typical store. I have here for comparison typical ratios based on a recent analysis made of the cost of doing business for dry goods and general merchandise stores.

"Now, Bill, here's how better control of costs might have increased your profits. Supposing you had held expenses to 27.1%, the level of the typical store. Your total expenses would have been only $50,885. Your net profit before taxes would have been increased from $1,311 to $10,892. That's enough to build an alcove, install the fixtures, and buy a good part of the new merchandise you'd need to fill the shelves."

"Gosh, if I only had that $9,500 extra profit! I see only two arrows pointing downward — the one for Mary's and my salary and the one for net profit."

"That's where your lack of cost control makes you take a licking, Bill. Before we analyze costs any further, let's see what you and Mary get out of all your effort. Look at partners' compensation: yours is only 5.4%, whereas the average for your line of business is 7.9%. And look at net profit of $1,311 before income tax: 0.7% against a typical net profit of 2.1%. Compensation and net profit represent your take from the business. Your take is well below average."

"That has me puzzled, Jack. I know we're selling more than ever before but I've never been so pinched for funds. Mary and I decided two years ago we'd have to draw a smaller salary until the expansion program was completed. But each year our take has been less and less."

"You're not alone, Bill. Lots of businessmen today face the same problem of holding costs in a more profitable ratio to net sales."

"What can I do about it? For all Mary and I do in this store we deserve at least the usual cut from the melon."

"From what I've seen of your business so far, Bill, you deserve more than the average. You have a very nice operation here. I can see you building your alcove in a short time and possibly opening a branch in Brookview in a few years. And perhaps with no further loans from the bank. Just from earnings kept in the business."

"Now you're talking my language, Jack. Yes, I see myself expanding into Brookview, too."

"But not before you get costs under control."

"Where do I begin?"

"You said you had budgeted sales at $160,000. Did you also budget costs?"

"No. We just tried to keep them as small as possible."

"We'll have to organize budgeting and record keeping better than that! I suggest we examine each item of your income statement. That way we can see where we can build profits, where we can reduce costs."

NET SALES

"Let's begin at the beginning with *Net Sales*. Your sales are increasing. But are you sure you are doing all you can to build sales even more? Could your clerks benefit from training to make them more effective sales people? Your talent, Bill, is selling. Why not pass along more of your successful selling techniques to the rest of your sales force? Have you considered setting up a prize incentive system or a bonus plan for your sales clerks?"

GROSS MARGIN

"You have a better than average *Gross Margin.** That's all in your favor. If we can find new ways to reduce merchandise costs further, you have that much more money for yourself and for operating expenses. With competition so keen today, it's important to buy from the right supplier who'll deliver quickly and who offers advantageous terms on special quantity purchases. Do you earn all discounts offered?"

"Sometimes. I would all the time if I had the money. Right now I have to count heavily on turnover to pay my bills. January is my worst month for sales. If some of my receivables come in more slowly than usual I may not have the cash to discount."

"Yet, if you took advantage of every possible discount, you'd reduce cost of goods and build gross margin.

"Now, Bill, before we take up each expense, I want to get this straight. It would be a mistake to assume we should try to reduce each cost item. In fact it may pay you to increase some of them. Control of costs is relative and results from a more profitable balance of individual costs. Perhaps you should spend more for such items as employee's incentives and advertising.

"Let's take a look now at your operating costs for last year. Some of these, such as rent, are fixed, though the rest of your occupancy expense may vary. Others, such as buying

See Appendix A for a convenient way to calculate mark-up and selling price to provide a desired gross margin.

expenses, are wholly variable. Fixed costs, as a percent of sales, can be reduced only by increasing net sales; the variable and semi-variable costs you can possibly reduce by limiting selectively the dollar amount spent. First of all, *Partners' Compensation.*"

"We don't want to cut that!"

EMPLOYEES' WAGES

"Of course not, Bill. But take *Employees' Wages.* Can you reduce anything there?"

"There may be a way. Alma Haine in the bedding section says she wants to retire April 1. Maybe I could get along without a replacement for Alma by shifting some personnel."

"That might cut the amount of dollars you pay out in wages. But let's look at this another way, Bill. You pay about $19,800 in wages. Dividing annual sales by that figure gives you about $9.50 in sales for every dollar of wages."

"Do you think I could increase that amount?"

"With training of your sales help, yes. You might step it up to $11 or $12 per dollar of wages. One way of doing that is to be sure your employees are the best you can hire for the wages you and your competitors pay. That means knowing your local labor market and persuading the best people to come to you. It means checking their experience and their references carefully. And training them.

OCCUPANCY EXPENSE

"Next, let's look at your *Occupancy Expense*. The rent you pay is only $4,800 a year. That's not bad for such a big place right on Main Street."

"No, it isn't, Jack, but to keep this old place together and looking right is expensive. Modernization, repair, and maintenance, according to our lease, is up to me. That's where the rest of the $8,358 goes — in keeping the place cool in summer, warm in winter, and well-lighted."

"Perhaps you can cut down heating bills by checking loose window sashes, sealing storm windows with masking tape, and building a winter vestibule around the front door. That will trap some of the cold air. You face North."

"And a little East, right in the line of the winds that come down the valley. Yes, I've been thinking about recaulking some of the windows."

"How about your use of electricity? Your conditioner can be turned off before closing time during the summer; the coolness will continue for a while. In winter, most of your customers will come in wearing coats. You can keep your heat at a level lower than your home and still be comfortable. With a hot water system you have a residual heating effect, too. You can afford to cut the heat long before closing. At night a reduced temperature is sufficient; in the morning you can raise it again. I notice, too, you have an old, corrugated iron ceiling."

"It came with the building. If it were my own building I would recover the ceiling with insulating tile. But it's too big a project. The iron will last a few more decades."

"You might consider changing the color from gloomy blue-gray. That ceiling absorbs light rather than reflects it. It probably is the reason you have so much auxiliary lighting in this store. The globes you have here just don't create enough light."

"I've put the biggest bulbs into them, too."

"You can get the most illumination per dollar from fluorescent lighting. Your expensive bulbs and dark paint are among the many small costs which have built up your high occupancy expense."

BUYING EXPENSE

"Let's look now at *Buying Expense*. Who does the buying for Brady's?"

"Mary and I do it. Sometimes we take the station wagon down as far as Chicago to bring back merchandise. I find it pays on smaller items, particularly apparel."

"How much do you estimate it costs to make the trip in

gas, food, and hotel expenses? You must stay at least one night in the city. How many trips do you make each year?"

"Too much and too many. I pick up merchandise every two weeks or so. Mary reads the trade papers and keeps track of what merchandise is moving. So I go to get it. I pick up reorders sometimes, too. I don't want to lose any sales because I don't have the merchandise."

"That's a good policy. You carry rather small inventories for the volume you transact."

"Sure, I let my suppliers pay for storage."

"That's OK. But maybe the money you spend on your buying trips is more than you might spend if you estimated inventory needs more carefully in the first place. Too little inventory can lose you sales as well as increase buying and shipping expenses. The cheaper methods of transportation are usually the slowest but you won't have to pay a premium for speed if you plan your purchases accurately.

ADVERTISING

"Now, about *Advertising*," Jack continued.

"That's the great unknown around here. I know I pay a lot of money for advertising and I don't know if I'm getting the results I should."

"What about your newspaper advertising?"

"Sometimes during a sale a customer comes in with my ad in his hand. I guess the space I buy does me a lot of good. It's hard to count results, though.

"Mary also mails post-cards to our credit customers."

"That's advertising, too, Bill. But to control advertising expenses you should find out which effort brings the best response. Then concentrate your spending there. Tell me, how do you make your promotions get interest and action?"

"Last November I built two revolving Christmas trees: tall, green pyramids with shelves. Mary filled them with costume jewelry, perfumes and other bright, interesting gifts. They were priced about right for the gift you'd want to give an aunt who has everything. Mary persuaded me to let the newspaper run a drawing of the trees in my usual space. We did very well with that idea. But it was expensive."

"Why not use more of the free displays your suppliers are always ready to put in? You can be selective and choose the material which best fits your store's merchandising plans. And have you thought about cooperative advertising with your suppliers or community advertising with some of the other merchants in town?"

"No, I haven't, Jack. But it's a good idea. I'll do something about that as soon as I can."

"You might tell Mary, too, to look into the postage she

pays for her mailings. No need to use first-class mail in most cases. Personalized letters generally are more effective than post-cards. A letter sent third-class bulk mail* costs less than post-cards or a first-class letter. I gather you do quite a lot of advertising by mail."

"There are more than 2,000 on our customer list, Jack."

"That could mean a considerable savings each time you mail third-class instead of post-card or first-class."

"And we mail ten or a dozen times a year. I'll tell Mary about third-class mail. We might be able to save a few hundred dollars that way."

DEPRECIATION AND OTHER EXPENSES

"Now, Bill, let's take Depreciation and Other Expenses. I've written off $1,879 as this year's depreciation on fixtures. I've lumped together such things as insurance, breakage, pilferage, spoilage of display merchandise and maintenance expense. Some of these other expenses are unavoidable. Some things are bound to spoil, for example. On the other hand, *breakage* can be brought within reasonable bounds by being sure shelves are stocked neatly and securely and by encouraging all the store personnel to handle inventory more carefully.

"You're fairly well set up here for guarding against *pilfer-*

*Mailings, to qualify for third-class bulk mail rates, require a permit from the Post Office. Postal rates and rules have been changing lately; it is best to check with your local post-master for current regulations.

age. There are only a few doors customers can use. If you, your wife and your clerks keep an eye out for shoplifters, you can cut down the amount of inventory loss. You can't avoid some *spoilage* of dresses and goods by long exposure on display racks or in the window. But you can give faded goods away, once they're cleaned, to a needy family or to a charity bazaar. That builds goodwill and puts the material to use. And quantities of slow-moving merchandise which might spoil or discolor on the shelves can be moved by a well-timed sale.

"For *insurance* you ought to consult your agent about variable coverage. You keep your inventory low—that's a help. But your off-season coverage may still be too high.

BAD DEBT LOSSES

"And finally, Bill, your *Bad Debt Losses*. A store loses money through bad debts because credit is not extended carefully enough in the first place and, secondly, because it may lack a well-defined, effective collection policy. Over half your sales, Bill, are on credit terms. You must select your credit customers carefully. Be sure you have full identification, name, address, and bank reference. And follow through on these references."

"Mary can do that for me."

"Even then, a few of your carefully screened accounts may delay. You'll save yourself time and money by clearly defining your credit and collection policy when a customer opens a credit account. And then be sure to send him a monthly statement on time. Your card or revolving file will tell you when an account is running past due. You can send a tactful reminder, such as a duplicate bill or prompt note. Some stores freeze further credits until an account pays up; others are adding up to 1½% a month carrying charge on all credit accounts."

"That sounds like a good idea, Jack."

"We have now considered the major items on your *income statement* from net sales to net profit before taxes. Step by step I've suggested some ways to reduce certain of your expenses in order to bring them closer to typical operating ratios for your line. It's up to you, now, to reduce these costs throughout the year. Such a program of control will pay off for you in greater profits and a greater take for you and Mary from your business."

"I'm all for that."

"And now I'd like to show you how your *balance sheet* can point the way to sound management, control of costs, and greater profits. Whatever you do as manager of your business shows up in your balance sheet, too. It is even more apparent when you compare balance sheet items over a period of years. Take your problem of credit granting which we were talking about a moment ago. That shows up on your balance sheet in the left-hand column as the amount carried in accounts receivable.

Cash in Bank	$19,138
Accounts Receivable	26,083
Merchandise	26,540
Total Current Assets	71,761
Fixtures & Equip.	9,411
(Reserve for Depreciation of 2,542)	
Station Wagon	2,000
Deposits	410
Total	83,582

Accounts Payable		$29,973
Owing Bank (due within year)		3,240
Total Current Liabilities		33,213
Owing Bank (due in more than one year)		2,700
Net Worth Dec. 31, 196– (last year)	46,819	
Plus Reinvested Earnings	850	
to Dec. 31, 196–		
	47,669	
Net Worth Dec. 31, 196– (current year)		47,669
Total		83,582

"When I listed your assets and liabilities as of December 31, this year, I also summarized your statements for the three past years.

	December 31, Previous Year	December 31, Last Year	December 31, This Year
Current Assets	$46,440	$51,617	$71,761
Current Liabilities	6,471	12,201	33,213
Other Assets	6,143	7,552	11,821
Tangible Net Worth	45,319	46,819	47,669
Net Working Capital	39,969	39,416	38,548
Net Sales	92,651	115,660	187,770
Net Profit (before taxes)	2,463 (2.7%)	1,953 (1.7%)	1,311 (0.7%)

"You have accounts receivable of $26,083 listed on your balance sheet. And they are included in the $71,761 of current assets listed in the comparative figures. See how fast your assets and liabilities have increased during the past three years. But your net worth and working capital have not. Also, your sales are up but your profits are not keeping pace."

"It's my apparel department, Jack. The volume in apparel has more than tripled since I started to sell on credit. The people around here are prospering. So I encourage them to buy on thirty-day credit."

"And they apparently do, judging from the size of your receivables. Tell me, how are the collections coming in?"

"Fair. Most of my customers mean well, though."

"Mean well but apparently they're slow. It looks as if you have too much of your money in receivables. What's your Collection Period?"

"Come again?"

"What's your Collection Period?"

"You're way out beyond me, Jack. You'll have to tell me."

"All right, I will. Let's see how much you carry as receivables. $26,083. What's the split of your annual sales between cash and credit?"

"That I can answer. Mary has been keeping track for me.

Let's see. This book has it. No. It's the other one. Here we are. You'll have to check the book for totals, Jack."

"Total sales on open account: $105,725; cash: $82,045. Dividing $105,725 by 365 days in a year you have net credit sales per day of $289.82. Then dividing your receivables ($26,083) by $289.82 gives you a Collection Period of about 90 days.

"As a general rule of thumb, the Collection Period of any business selling merchandise on an open-book account should be no more than $\frac{1}{3}$ greater than net selling terms. In this case, since your open account selling terms are net 30 days, you should have a Collection Period of no longer than 40 days. *Yours is more than twice that long.* By letting receivables slow down this way, you encourage accounts to delay.

"The longer they delay, the bigger are the chances they won't pay at all. Your income statement showed a bad debt loss of $3,193, more than twice your net profit. You ought to determine immediately the age of each of your accounts.

"Now," Jack continued, "there are a few other things your balance sheet can tell us. Dun & Bradstreet sent me these financial ratios* which are comparisons of various items on your balance sheet and income statement. Collection

*Dun & Bradstreet computes each year 14 Important Ratios from an analysis of balance sheets in 72 lines of business (manufacturing, wholesale, and retail). Single copies of the 14 Important Ratios are available free on request. Address Dun & Bradstreet, Inc., Business Publications Division, P.O. Box 803, Church Street Station, New York 8, New York.

Period is a ratio we've already discussed. Here are five other important ratios. I've figured yours and put beside them, for comparison, typical ratios for the line."

	Financial Ratios of Brady's	Typical Financial Ratios for the Line
I Current Assets to Current Debt	↓ 2.2 times	6.3 times
II Net Profit on Tangible Net Worth	↓ 2.7%	7.2%
III Net Sales to Tangible Net Worth	↑ 3.9 times	2.4 times
IV Net Sales to Net Working Capital	↑ 4.9 times	3.0 times
V Current Debt to Tangible Net Worth	↑ 69.7%	16.2%

"I see you've used arrows again."

"Yes, they show four things: (1) your current ratio of assets to liabilities is low, only 2.2 times; (2) your profit is low in comparison with your investment; (3) you turn over your net worth and net working capital faster than usual; and (4) your debt is heavier than the debt typically carried by businesses in your line.

"Your long Collection Period is a symptom of your heavy receivables. Your large debt, as shown by the ratio of Current Debt to Tangible Net Worth, can affect your credit standing and your position with the suppliers who can offer you the best service and merchandise. Suppose a manufacturer, closing out a line, offered you a substantial discount on an attractive group of dresses if you could pay cash. Could you take advantage of the offer without special financing? I doubt it, Bill."

"You certainly are right, Jack."

"You said January was your dullest month for sales. I've taken that into consideration. Here's roughly what you'll have coming in and going out between now, January 3, and the end of the month.

EXPECTED CASH FOR JANUARY

Cash on Hand and in the Bank.................................$19,100
Cash Income 12,500
   (including expected sales for cash and collection of receivables)
                                                                   $31,600

MUST PAY IN JANUARY

Bills $30,000
Owing Bank 270
   (monthly amount)
Expenses 4,230
   (including partners' drawings, wages, advertising, occupancy, other)
                                                                $34,500

"It looks to me as if you're not going to have enough cash at the end of January to pay everything due then."

"Some of those bills are due March 1. I'd say only about $27,000 of that $30,000 is due by February 1."

"It's still going to be tight for you, Bill. Your best bet is to concentrate this month on collecting past due accounts. Then you'll have the cash to meet your bills. And you might be able to earn more discounts and take advantage of some manufacturers' January clearance sales for cash.

"So you see, Bill, how your balance sheet has given us a way to help you build profits by controlling costs. We traced the effect of heavy receivables on your cash position. I've shown you a way to keep track each month of your expected cash intake and outgo. Many progressive businessmen project their cash position months in advance. Then they follow through with positive action. This control results in sufficient cash to cover normal costs and gives the businessman money to use when advantageous buying opportunities come along.

"Let's look into the months ahead, Bill. By way of summary, here's what you should do to build your profits by controlling costs:

1. Keep your sales moving up as you have been.
2. Watch your average gross margin. Keep control of markdowns. Earn discounts when offered.
3. Cut down variable operating expenses wherever possible.
4. Go ahead with a collection clean-up campaign.
5. Be more selective about extending new credit.
6. Keep accurate records. Study them frequently to see how well you've kept costs in line. And call me whenever you have a question or a problem."

"That does it, Jack. The alcove will have to wait until I put in order the business I already have. The way Mary and I work we deserve to enjoy all the profits we can earn."

"I couldn't agree with you more."

"Jack, you're the best investment I'll make this year. I just didn't realize mere figures could tell me so quickly where I was goofing in the management of my business."

That's the story of Bill Brady and how he learned to build profits by controlling costs. Does your firm have a project in mind? If it does, have you closely analyzed your balance sheets to control costs? If so, what have you done?

_____

_____

_____

_____

_____

_____

_____

_____

CHAPTER 3

What Your Financial
Statement Can Tell You

"He that delights in his trade will delight in his books; and,
as I have already laid it down for a rule, that he who will
thrive must diligently attend his shop or warehouse, and
take up his delight here, so I say now he must also diligently keep his books, or else he will never know whether
he thrives or not."

From The Compleat English Tradesman
Daniel Defoe, 1726

Bill Brady learned much from Jack Larkin's analysis of
his business. If he follows the suggestions his accountant
made, his business could grow into a very profitable and
satisfying enterprise. But Jack Larkin or any consultant
cannot make suggestions such as these when a business
fails to keep adequate records. The only possible way to
control profits is to continually analyze all factors. This
is simple, sound business management. From the daily and
monthly records, financial statements are prepared and
the health of your business determined.

Throughout our years of working with businesses of all types and sizes, Dun & Bradstreet has learned that the absence of adequate records is one of the major reasons for failure. Many of the men and women who failed in the past decade did not have adequate information about their operations. Many just didn't know where their dollars were being lost.

HOW TO GET THE FACTS

Getting the figures is simple. All it takes is a formalized accounting system based on the needs of the type, size and complexity of the business. A retail store run by a family will require fewer records than does a department store. A small electronics parts maker needs less than does an industrial giant.

The proprietor of a typical small store, for example, should keep records which will answer the following questions. Try to answer them if you fit in this category.

How much business (cash and charge) am I doing?

How much am I collecting on my charge business?

How much do my customers owe me now (both current and past due), and can I stand this much?

How much cash do I have on hand and in the bank? Is this the amount I should have on hand or is there any cash shortage?

How much stock (inventory) do I have on hand?

How much merchandise do I take out of my store for personal use which I do not consider as sales?

How much do I owe my wholesalers and others?

How much gross margin did I earn?

How much were my expenses?

How much net profits (if any) did I earn? How much income taxes will I have to pay?

What is my net worth; that is, what is the amount of my proprietorship in the store?

What are the trends in my sales, expenses, profits, net worth, etc.; that is, how is my store progressing from year to year?

How does my store compare with other stores in the same line of business?

Your own needs can best be determined by consulting your accountant or another consultant, a trade association, or a supplier. You should know what is the basis of a financial management program. This book will outline the subject.

Even the most skillful drivers need a rear-view mirror to help them reach their destination. In business, your rear-view mirrors are the profit and loss sheet and the balance sheet. They will show you what you have made and also answer many other important questions for you, just as they did for Bill Brady in our last chapter.

THE PROFIT AND LOSS SHEET

We've seen that income is traced from sales minus the cost of goods to gross profit; then minus operating expenses to net profit or take home pay. On paper this technique is called developing the profit and loss statement. It is the first step for a consultant like Jack Larkin when he begins to measure a business.

THE BALANCE SHEET

The Profit and Loss Statement does not, however, give you the complete story. The profits shown are just paper profits until you know where the money is. You cannot tell how healthy your business really is until a balance sheet is prepared. This shows what money is in your bank accounts and how much is tied up in inventory, equipment, plant or fixtures, and accounts receivable.

The balance sheet reveals a firm's assets and liabilities. It cannot show you if your business has been profitable, but it does show where you stand at a given moment in a year.

Every practice or action of management is reflected somewhere in your records. Here are typical problems that a manager will find when he looks for leaks:

1. The careless granting of credit will be shown on your balance sheet by swollen receivables and probably by a long collection period.
2. Your own purchases of merchandise or raw materials in excess of demand will be shown in larger inventories and a slowing rate of turnover.
3. If you have expanded your business, this will appear as an increase in fixed assets.

Features of your balance sheet will influence items on your income statement. For example:

1. If receivables are heavy and include a large number of past due or doubtful accounts, a charge off for bad debts greater than anticipated will diminish profits.
2. If inventory is top-heavy and prices fall, it will be necessary to write down the inventory. This may entirely wipe out your profits.
3. If fixed assets are excessive, the annual depreciation charges can become a heavy demand against income.
4. If it is necessary to borrow in large amounts, the interest will eat into profits.

5. Management's decisions on dividends or withdrawals of money by partners or proprietors affect the final amount of net profit added to a business's net worth.

Most businessmen can tell you their approximate net sales, gross margin and net profit from their latest income statement. A smaller number can tell of individual expense items and whether these are better, typical, or worse than the usual figures for a successful business in their line. But very few businessmen make use of their balance sheet as a tool for control. Both the balance sheet and income statement, when their elements are understood and intelligently compared, can yield valuable information for controlling costs.

To analyze your financial records you should use a tool called "Ratio Analysis." Chapter 5 will show you how you figure your operating and financial ratios. First, let's see in Chapter 4 how we can set up a cost control program.

Organizing for Cost Control

Controlling expenses means that you determine your expenses over the past few years, determine what they should be for the coming year and set up controls to see that you live within your expenses. Doing these things is well worth your time because you are forced to become conscious of costs.

With an accounting system set up specifically for your business you have the figures to show what your business is doing. You can compare each month, each quarter and each year with the same period in earlier years and with other firms in your line of business.

The discovery of lost profits is not going to make more money for you automatically. You must make definite plans to control your future operations—to spend each dollar so it will bring in more business or greater profit.

BUDGETING BECOMES IMPORTANT

To do this you must budget sales, gross profit and expenses in advance. This will help you predict whether or not the profit at the end of any period will be satisfactory. Then when that period is over, you can see just how close you came to your budget. You will also be able to see how well you are staying on target by checking yourself as you move towards your goal.

Controlling expenses causes you to figure in advance which expense level will give you the best results. This will make you aware that any expenses in excess of your budget come directly out of your profits.

Should business fall below your expectations, you'll know just when and where you can trim expenses. When business exceeds your expectations, you'll be able to keep a firm hand on your business to eliminate unnecessary waste and to increase profits.

MAKING A SALES FORECAST

The first step in controlling money is to set up a sales forecast. Here you predict all your income. To do this you should use all available information from industry, local business conditions, and your own experience.

Now estimate your expected sales. Some companies do this by charting their sales expectations on graph paper, beginning with the trend they have established during the past three or five years. Always remember in your planning that your sales objectives should be kept in line with your own ability to meet demand.

Once you feel your forecast for the coming years shows a proper extension of your company's trend, weigh your estimate against current conditions in your market area or business line. Be sure to take into consideration such factors as competition of all types for the consumer's dollar.

Once you have arrived at a final estimate of your next year's sales, break it down by month according to average monthly percentages of expected business. These should be based on your past two or three year's experience. You will now be able to check your progress at the end of each month, each quarter and the entire year. Whenever you find your progress below expectations, you must take action to bring in more business, or to cut expenses in line with lower income.

In any business, price level expenses, sales costs, financing and other factors are related to sales. That is why this sales forecast is the starting point of a cost control program.

As you prepare such other controls as expense budgets and cost budgets, you may find it necessary to revise the sales forecast. This is the normal part of budgeting so that all phases of a business will balance. When this point is reached, your business will be geared to the most economical use of labor, materials, facilities and capital.

The cash budget is an important companion to the sales budget. It helps you carefully plan the use of money during any given period. To make it a success you must decide in advance what to do about: increases in fixed assets, increases in inventory, amount of accounts receivable, long term financing and short term financing.

The expense budget is a control to help you oversee your operations. Many companies base their expense budget on their previous three or five years. They compute their average expense for each area of operations and determine what percentage of gross sales these averages represent. Each percentage is multiplied by our forecasted sales budget. This provides what is often called a "mechanical budget." This is checked each month to see how closely you are staying to your price and expenses so that you can come up with the gross and net profits you need to prosper.

HEART OF FINANCIAL MANAGEMENT

Budgets are the heart of financial planning and control. When you prepare them you can be sure that:

1. You direct your capital into the best short-term and long-term channels.

2. You carefully think through the proper use of unused depreciation and maintenance funds.

3. You prevent waste in different departments and areas of your company.

4. You clearly establish responsibility for each function of your business.

5. You compel all departments to cooperate to achieve company goals.

6. You have a safety signal which quickly indicates variations between estimates and actual results.

7. You have a tool for conservation of resources since spending is kept within the confines of income.

8. You must develop an adequate accounting and record program.

9. You are compelled to study your markets, products and services and methods, and thus point up ways to enlarge your business.

10. You develop a well-ordered budget plan. This will put your company in a far more advantageous position if you must deal with banks or other financial sources.

When you have prepared a budget, what you have done actually is to set up a target to shoot at, and a measuring device to check your accuracy.

It is the test of good management to make things happen in accordance with a well-ordered plan. To do this, it is vitally important to put your profit improvement program on a team basis. If your firm is small you can gather all your employees together and tell them your problem. If it is large, you talk to the men and women who influence selling, pricing, costs and operations, and leave the communication problem to them.

In either case you work out yourself, or with others what you consider a fair gross margin of profit as a target. Encourage all personnel to help make profit improvement a way of life for your business.

The true knowledge of figures, the setting of yardsticks, the use of controls and a joint team effort will result in greater profits.

Which employees and executives influence most heavily profit improvement in your business? Develop a cost control committee from this knowledge. Whom do you invite to sit on this committee? _____

_____

_____

_____

_____

_____

_____

_____

_____

_____

CHAPTER 5

How To Figure Your Operating And Financial Ratios

If you are like most businessmen, you will want to know not only where profit leaks are located, but also how you compare with other companies in your line of business. Comparing net profits is not always the best way to do this. This kind of comparison tells nothing about the relative efficiencies of managements, or the money needed to make a profit.

Your banker and accountant have some definite methods of measurement. We call it "ratio analysis." Let's see how Jack Larkin was able to give Bill Brady such a comprehensive picture of his business in Chapter 2.

OPERATING RATIOS

Operating ratios are comparisons between individual items found for the most part on an income statement. They are expressed as a percent; for example, so many dollars of advertising expense per 100 dollars of net sales.

A ratio is easily found through simple division of one item by another.

Items used in figuring ratios are explained in alphabetical order on the following pages. Several examples of calculations are given to help you make your own. After the explanations there is a handy chart with four spaces where you can (1) enter your budgeted dollar amounts and the percent of net sales they represent; (2) enter your actual performance; (3) enter typical ratios for your line. See pages 55 to 63 for operating and financial ratios.

ADVERTISING
Net expenditure for newspaper, direct mail, and other forms of advertising exclusive of wages.

BAD DEBT LOSSES
Receivables considered during the year as uncollectible or the reserve set up to cover such losses.

BUYING EXPENSE
Cost of travel for buying purposes or commissions paid to buying organizations.

COST OF GOODS SOLD
Opening inventory plus merchandise purchased (including inbound freight and cartage but deducting cash discounts received) less closing inventory.

Example

```
OPENING  INVENTORY  ........................................$ 8,800
ADD  MERCHANDISE  PURCHASED  .....................  26,200
PLUS  FREIGHT  CHARGES  ............................      525
                                               26,725    26,725
                                                         35,525
LESS  CASH  DISCOUNTS  ......................................  275
                                                         35,250
DEDUCT  CLOSING  INVENTORY  ...............................  8,200
COST  OF  GOODS  SOLD  ......................................  27,050
```

YOUR FIGURES

$. . . . .

. . . .
. . . .
. . . .

. . . .
. . . .
. . . .
. . . .
. . . .
. . . .

↑

Cost of Goods Sold

DEPRECIATION ON FIXTURES

Amounts charged during the year to depreciation on store fixtures and equipment.

EMPLOYEES' WAGES

Gross payroll of all employees including amount withheld for income taxes.

EXPENSE, ALL OTHER

Residue of miscellaneous expense items, such as store supplies, telephone, professional service, donations; also, all taxes except property, income, excise, and sales taxes.

GROSS MARGIN

The difference between net sales and cost of goods sold, also known as gross profit on sales. Even in a single store this is a composite figure: the net result of selling different kinds of goods at varying mark-ups. Cash discounts received, where any were earned, are treated as a reduction of cost of goods.

Example

```
NET SALES .............................................$40,575
COST OF GOODS SOLD.................................... 27,050
GROSS MARGIN .........................................$13,525
```

YOUR FIGURES

$....................................

....

$....................................

↑

Gross Margin

INVENTORY TURNOVER

Cost of goods sold divided by average inventory (average of opening and closing inventories).

Example

```
OPENING INVENTORY .......................$8,800
CLOSING INVENTORY .......................  8,200
                              2 ) 17,000 = 8,500
                                   Average Inventory
                                   3.18 or 3.2 times per year
```

3.18 times

AVERAGE INVENTORY ....$8,500) $27,050.00 Cost of Goods Sold

YOUR FIGURES

$................

....
2) ....

....
times
per year

$................) $................

NET PROFIT BEFORE INCOME TAXES

The difference between gross margin and total expense before deduction for Federal and State income taxes, but after allowance for owners' or partners' salaries.

Example

GROSS MARGIN $13,525

TOTAL EXPENSE 12,922
(Including Owners' Salaries)

NET PROFIT BEFORE INCOME TAXES...........................$ 603

YOUR FIGURES

$.............................

....
$.............................Net Profit

NET SALES

Gross sales less returns and allowances and less excise and sales taxes collected; net after all discounts.

Example

GROSS SALES $42,329

LESS RETURN ALLOWANCES...................................   410

                                                         41,919

LESS 3% SALES TAX.. 1,344

NET SALES $40,575

YOUR FIGURES

$............................

....

....

....

$............................Net Sales

(NOTE: Sales Tax collected exceeds 3% because of fractions of $1)

NET WORTH

The difference between total assets and total liabilities; in a corporation, the sum of capital stock and earned or paid in surplus.

Example

TOTAL ASSETS $15,922

LESS—CURRENT LIABILITIES 1,522

LESS—DEFERRED LIABILITIES 1,000   2,522

NET WORTH $13,400

YOUR FIGURES

$..................

....

....

Net Worth $..................

OCCUPANCY EXPENSE

The expense of occupying a building, whether rented or owned. For renters this item includes rent, utilities, and leasehold improvements; for owners it includes utilities, property insurance, property taxes, building depreciation, and interest on mortgage.

OWNERS' COMPENSATION

Salaries or drawings of proprietors, partners, or officers.

TOTAL EXPENSE

The sum of all individual expense items.

TYPICAL RATIO

The "median" selected by arranging the performance ratios in a particular group in order of size and taking the ratio halfway down the list. The median is therefore typical in the sense that half of the reported or computed figures in a given group are higher than the median and half are lower.

FINANCIAL RATIOS

Financial ratios are simple comparisons between items on a balance sheet and income statement. They can be found by dividing one item by another.

Financial ratios, like operating ratios, describe what has happened to a business during the period covered by a statement. They cannot tell why it has happened, however, nor can they predict the future. Rather, they are convenient warnings which point out where additional investigation and possible action are necessary. Ratios yield their most valuable information when studied over a period of years for their trend.

Following the explanation of some individual financial ratios on the following pages is a comparative five year chart on which you can enter your balance sheet figures, your operating or income figures, and financial ratios.

CURRENT ASSETS TO CURRENT DEBTS

This is often known as the current ratio. It is found by dividing current assets by current liabilities. *Current assets* represent the total of cash, accounts and notes receivable for the sale of merchandise in regular trade quarters less any reserves, inventory, listed securities when not in excess of market, state and municipal bonds not in excess of market, and United States Government securities. *Current debt* represents the total of all liabilities due within one year from the statement date. This item also includes reserves such as gross reserves for Federal income and excess profits taxes and reserves for contingencies set up for specific purposes, but it does not include reserves for depreciation.

Example

CURRENT LIABILITIES ....$35,000) $70,000 Current Assets

2 Current Ratio

YOUR FIGURES

$................) $................

Current Ratio

Maxim: For years businessmen have judged, as a rule of thumb, that a current ratio of at least 2 (that is, current assets worth twice as much as current liabilities) showed a healthy business. Nowadays, however, this ratio can vary wth safety, depending on the line of business and the length of time in business.

NET PROFIT ON NET SALES

In this fundamental ratio, *net* profits represent profits after full depreciation on buildings, machinery, equipment, furniture, and other assets of a fixed nature; after reserves for Federal income and excess profits taxes; after reduction in the value of inventory to cost or market, whichever is lower; after charge-offs for bad debts; after miscellaneous reserves and adjustments; but before dividends or withdrawals. Net sales represent the dollar volume of business for a year after deductions for returns, allowances, and discounts from gross sales.

Example
↓   .034 or 3.4%

NET SALES ....$135,293) $4,600.00

YOUR FIGURES

or   %

$...............) $...............

This ratio can vary widely depending on the line of business. Certain businesses, such as manufacturers of chemicals, tend toward fairly large profits on each dollar of sales. Others, such as wholesalers of cigars, cigarettes, and tobacco, generally show small profits on sales. Although profits are the goal of a business, an enterprise cannot be operated only for maximum short term profits at the expense of financial health. If net profits are unusually large, it is necessary to determine whether they resulted from temporary economic factors which gave sales and profits a boost or whether they resulted from normal but very efficient operations under the guidance of unusually capable management.

NET PROFIT ON TANGIBLE NET WORTH

This ratio represents return on the investment in the business. It complements the ratio of net profit on net sales. In calculating this ratio, *tangible net worth* represents the sum of all outstanding stock, surplus, and undivided profits (in the case of a corporation) or net worth (in the case of a proprietor or partnership) less any intangible items in the assets, such as goodwill, trademarks, patents, copyrights, leaseholds, mailing lists, treasury stock, organization expenses, and underwriting discounts and expenses.

Example
↓   .085 or 8.5%
TANGIBLE NET WORTH....................$54,117) $4,600.00 Net Profit

YOUR FIGURES

                                             or   %
$................) $................

Businesses showing the highest percentage net profit on tangible net worth and on net sales, not for a single year but over a sustained period of time, are naturally the most highly regarded. Either their managements have done a better job or the concerns are in a line with a favorable growth and operating position.

NET SALES TO TANGIBLE NET WORTH

This ratio indicates the activity of the investment in a business.

Example

      ↓   2.5 times

TANGIBLE NET WORTH .... $54,117) $135,293.00 Net Sales

YOUR FIGURES

                                               times

$...............) $...............

Maxim: Probably more businesses undertrade on their investment than overtrade. But overtrading can be alarming to creditors. Generally speaking, a business is seriously overtrading if this ratio is more than twice as large as the typical ratio for its line.

NET SALES TO NET WORKING CAPITAL

This ratio complements the ratio of net sales to tangible net worth. The two ratios will usually follow parallel trends if fixed or slow assets are normal for the line.

Example

      ↓   3.1 times

NET WORKING CAPITAL .... $43,810) $135,293.00 Net Sales

YOUR FIGURES

                                               times

$...............) $...............

If this ratio is excessive in comparison to others in your line, and the ratio of net sales to tangible net worth is normal for the line, there is probably an unusually large investment in fixed or slow assets.

CURRENT DEBT TO TANGIBLE NET WORTH

This ratio contrasts the funds which creditors are temporarily risking in a business with the funds invested in the business by the owners.

Example
↓

TANGIBLE NET WORTH ....$54,117 $\overline{) \text{ \$35,000.00 Current Debt}}$ .646 or 64.6%

YOUR FIGURES

$\overline{\text{or \quad \%}}$
$.................) $.................

Heavy current liabilities in comparison with tangible net worth always signal a need for close analysis.

COLLECTION PERIOD

Computing this ratio we get the number of days represented by the total of trade accounts and notes receivable (including assigned accounts and discounted notes, if any, less reserves for bad debts) when compared with the annual net credit sales. This ratio is convenient for determining the health of a company's receivables as of statement date. The Collection Period (P) can be found easily by using this formula: $P = \dfrac{r}{d}$

in which *r* represents accounts receivable plus notes receivable (including discounted notes receivable) and *d* represents net credit sales per day (net credit sales for one year divided by 365).

Example ↓

$$\begin{array}{r} \$315 \text{ Net Credit Sales per day} \\ \hline 365 \overline{)\ \$115{,}000 \text{ Net Credit Sales per year}} \end{array}$$

$$P = r = \frac{9765}{315} \text{ or 31 days}$$
$$ d 315$$

YOUR FIGURES:

$$\begin{array}{r} \\ \hline 365 \overline{)\ \$\dots\dots\dots\dots\ \dots} \end{array} \qquad \begin{array}{r} \text{days} \\ \hline \overline{)\ \$\dots\dots\dots\dots} \end{array}$$

Maxim: The Collection Period should be no more than one-third greater than the net selling terms of a particular business enterprise normally selling its merchandise on open book account. That means a concern selling on 2-10-net 30 days terms should have a Collection Period no greater than 30 plus $\dfrac{30}{3}$, or 40 days.

CHART FOR COMPUTING AND COMPARING
YOUR OPERATING RATIOS

	YOUR BUDGET		YOUR ACTUAL OPERATING RESULTS		Typical Ratios for Your Line*
		Per-cent of Net Sales		Per-cent of Net Sales	Per-cent of Net Sales
NET SALES	$	100%	$	100%	100%
COST OF GOODS SOLD					
GROSS MARGIN					
EXPENSES**					
Owners' (or Partners') Compensation					
Employees' Wages					
Occupancy Expenses					
Advertising					
Bad Debt Losses					
Buying Expense					
Depreciation, Fixtures					
Supplies					
Delivery Expense					
Laundry, Dry Cleaning					
Replacements					
Licenses and Permits					
All Other Expense					
TOTAL EXPENSE					
NET PROFIT BEFORE INCOME TAXES					

Inventory Turnover (Times)

*See ratios on pages 78 to 121 for typical operating figures which you can use for comparison.

**Fill in only those expense items which apply to your line of business.

YOUR FINANCIAL STATEMENT

BALANCE

STATEMENT DATE		
Cash		
Notes Receivable		
Accounts Receivable		
Inventory		
TOTAL CURRENT ASSETS		
Land		
Fixtures, Equipment		
Other Fixed Assets		
TOTAL ASSETS		

A FIVE-YEAR COMPARISON

SHEET

Continued

58

YOUR FINANCIAL STATEMENT

BALANCE

Due Banks		
Accounts Payable		
Federal Income Taxes		
TOTAL CURRENT LIABILITIES		
PREFERRED STOCK		
COMMON STOCK		
PAID IN SURPLUS		
CAPITAL SURPLUS		
NET WORTH (Proprietors or Partners)		
TOTAL LIABILITIES AND CAPITAL		
NET WORKING CAPITAL		
TANGIBLE NET WORTH		
NET SALES		
NET PROFIT		
Dividends or Withdrawals		
Res. for Depreciation		
Res. for Bad Debts		

A FIVE-YEAR COMPARISON

SHEET *Continued*

INCOME STATEMENT • NET WORTH

STATEMENT DATE		% of Net Sales	Typical % for Line		% of Net Sales	Typical % for Line
		100%	100%		100%	100%
COST OF GOODS SOLD						
GROSS PROFIT (LOSS) ON SALES						
EXPENSES Owners' Compensation						
Employees' Wages						
Occupancy Expense						
Advertising						
Bad Debt Loss						
Buying Expense						
Depreciation, Fixtures						
All Other Expense						
NET INCOME (LOSS) ON SALES						
OTHER INCOME						
OTHER EXPENSES						
NET INCOME (LOSS) BEFORE TAXES						
Federal Income Taxes						
Other Taxes on Income						

RECONCILIATION • FINANCIAL RATIOS

	% of Net Sales	Typical % for Line		% of Net Sales	Typical % for Line		% of Net Sales	Typical % for Line
	100%	100%		100%	100%		100%	100%

Continued

INCOME STATEMENT • NET WORTH

NET INCOME (LOSS) AFTER TAXES				
Adjustments—Add				
Adjustments—Deduct				
NET INCOME (LOSS) AS ADJUSTED				
SURPLUS OR NET WORTH AT START				
ADDITIONS Adjusted Net Income				
DEDUCTIONS Adjusted Net Loss				
Dividends—Withdrawals				
SURPLUS OR NET WORTH AT END				

	My Business	Typical	My Business	Typical
Current Assets to Current Debt	Times	Times	Times	Times
Net Profit on Net Sales	%	%	%	%
Net Profit on Tangible Net Worth	%	%	%	%
Net Sales to Tangible Net Worth	Times	Times	Times	Times
Net Sales to Net Working Capital	Times	Times	Times	Times
Collection Period	Days	Days	Days	Days
Inventory Turnover	Times	Times	Times	Times
Current Debt to Tangible Net Worth	%	%	%	%

RECONCILIATION • FINANCIAL RATIOS *Continued*

My Business	Typical	My Business	Typical	My Business	Typical
My Business	Typical	My Business	Typical	My Business	Typical
Times	Times	Times	Times	Times	Times
%	%	%	%	%	%
%	%	%	%	%	%
Times	Times	Times	Times	Times	Times
Times	Times	Times	Times	Times	Times
Days	Days	Days	Days	Days	Days
Times	Times	Times	Times	Times	Times
%	%	%	%	%	%

CHAPTER 6

A Cost Control Check List
for Smaller Businesses

The goal of any business, large or small, is to make a profit. Profits are the evidence of management capacity. Management is the art of controlling and directing men and materials toward the goal of profits.

An expanding economy tends to make this art easier, but a period of adversity quickly exposes weaknesses in a manager's control.

The most successful managements know they can build their rate of profit easily when sales climb. But, with skill, they have found they can also build it when sales remain on a plateau and even when volume slides. They accomplish this feat by building their gross margin or controlling their costs (frequently by both methods in varying combinations). Herein lies the strong, individual talent of a successful manager. Through fat and lean economies he consistently carries a rewarding part of the sales dollar down to the finish line as net profit.

After doing what he can about sales, a manager controls costs by finding out where the business seems to be getting out of line compared with past performance and compared with the performance of others. He carries out this self analysis with a healthy skepticism for "average" or "typical" performance. The most successful managers, after all, surpass what is average or usual.

When a business compares unfavorably with typical ratios, however, this warning signal should be taken to heart. It is then necessary to investigate more closely those areas where operations seem to generate excessive costs.

Possible areas where lack of control may hinder profit building are management records, cost of goods, owners' compensation, employees' wages, occupancy expense, advertising, credit (or bad debt losses), buying, and such other expenses as depreciation, insurance, etc. As a manager examines each area of costs he can ask himself the following ten general questions about each activity which contributes to specific costs:

1. What is the purpose of the activity?
2. Why is it necessary?
3. When is it done?
4. Where is it done?
5. Who should do it?
6. How should it be done?
7. How many use the result of the activity?
8. Can it be eliminated?
9. Can it be combined with another operation?
10. Can it be improved through rearrangement?

The questions on the following pages were prepared to indicate practical ways to cut costs or to get better value for money spent.

Here's how you can quickly check your own operations:

if you can answer *yes* to a question, make a check mark in the box under YES. If you can't say *yes* wholeheartedly, make a check mark in the box under NO. When you have finished, if you have checked some NO's, you may want to consider whether you can benefit from the practical action suggested by the question.

These questions are by no means all which can be asked. An outside business advisor, such as your accountant, major supplier, bank, or trade organization, or an article in a trade or business magazine can suggest other points tailor-made to your individual business or line.

MANAGEMENT RECORDS

YES NO

☐ ☐ Have I set up a budget of costs based on the sales, gross profit, and net profit I consider my year's goal?

☐ ☐ Have I determined what records I must keep in order to know quickly when my costs are out of line?

☐ ☐ Have I compared my operating and financial ratios with those of preceding years and with typical ratios for my line?

☐ ☐ Do I compare actual costs with the budget and find reasons for differences?

☐ ☐ Do I have a written estimate of expected sales, costs, material and personnel needed, based on

YES NO

a projection of expected profits for a month, a
year, three years?

COST OF GOODS

☐ ☐   Do I earn all purchase discounts offered me by
my suppliers?

☐ ☐   Do I have sufficient cash on hand and in the
bank to take advantage of special offers of merchandise at reduced prices if paid for in cash?

☐ ☐   Do I review my merchandise periodically to
weed out old stock for quick sale?

☐ ☐   Do I have a clear understanding with my suppliers about who pays freight expenses for goods
shipped?

☐ ☐   Have I recently compared freight rates for different kinds of transportation?

OWNERS' COMPENSATION

☐ ☐   Does my annual take (my salary plus net profit)
figured as a percent of my investment in my
business, give me a satisfying return compared
with other ways I might invest my talent?

☐ ☐   Have I reviewed my business with my account-

YES NO

ant to determine if some other form of legal organization might not yield a higher net return on my investment?

EMPLOYEES' WAGES

☐ ☐ Are the people I employ generally as high or higher in calibre as those my competitors employ?

☐ ☐ Do I train my employees so they improve in capability, efficiency, and customer relations?

☐ ☐ Have I a working system and wage rate which encourage employees to work most effectively?

☐ ☐ Have I studied the turnover rate of my personnel?

☐ ☐ Do I know the cost to me of overtime payments?

☐ ☐ Do I explain what is required of an employee when he is assigned a job and do I then follow through to see if the assignment is carried out effectively?

☐ ☐ Am I familiar with the sources for obtaining personnel needed in my business?

☐ ☐ Do I check personnel references thoroughly?

YES NO

☐ ☐ Do I review personnel procedures periodically to take advantage of changes in applicable laws?

OCCUPANCY EXPENSE

☐ ☐ Have I recently checked my mechanical equipment to see whether it needs preventive maintenance?

☐ ☐ Have I checked my heating or cooling system to be sure it is shut off when not actually needed?

☐ ☐ Have I made provision for the most economical servicing of my operating equipment?

ADVERTISING

☐ ☐ Is my merchandise attractively displayed both on the shelves and in my windows?

☐ ☐ Do I tell established customers by newspaper or direct mail when special sales or seasonal merchandise promotions are planned? Do I take advantage of bulk-rate, third-class postage, when feasible, for direct mail promotions? Do I regularly revise my lists?

☐ ☐ Do I measure my advertising results against my

advertising investment, where possible, in order to determine the efficiency of various methods of advertising and promotion?

CREDIT

☐ ☐ Have I made clear to my credit customers exactly what my credit and collection policy is?

☐ ☐ Do I systematically check new applicants for credit to be sure they are worthy of being sold on open account terms?

☐ ☐ Should I offer an incentive, such as refund of a carrying charge, to customers who pay promptly?

BUYING

☐ ☐ Do I buy merchandise items in quantities which meet customer demand quite closely?

☐ ☐ Do I watch carefully to be sure I'm buying from suppliers who can give me the best service, the fastest delivery, as well as reasonable prices?

☐ ☐ Do I know alternate sources of supply?

☐ ☐ Am I familiar with price movements of the different items I purchase?

YES NO

☐ ☐ Do I buy in economical lots which offer me a chance for maximum profit per unit, and at the same time do I avoid overstocking?

☐ ☐ Am I familiar with the quality of merchandise offered me by suppliers?

☐ ☐ Do I inspect shipments as soon as they arrive?

☐ ☐ If someone buys for me, do I frequently review the performance of that buyer?

OTHER EXPENSES

☐ ☐ If the difference between replacement and depreciated value of my fixtures is great, have I made adequate reserves for eventual replacement?

☐ ☐ Do I keep a record of all small, miscellaneous expenses such as the telephone bill and messengers?

☐ ☐ Do I vary my insurance depending on seasonal levels of merchandise?

☐ ☐ Have I worked out a way to reduce soiling and spoiling of inventory?

☐ ☐ Once it is spoiled or soiled, have I worked out a way to salvage part of its cost?

YES NO

☐ ☐ Have I reviewed my method of depreciation with an outside advisor to be sure it offers the maximum tax relief to my business?

☐ ☐ Would I be better off leasing some of my fixtures and equipment instead of owning them?

☐ ☐ Do I spend too much for such customer services as repairs and deliveries?

AN OUTSIDE ADVISER

☐ ☐ Do I have someone outside my business, such as an accountant, banker, or business friend, review my business operation from time to time?

☐ ☐ Do I regularly read a trade magazine and a business management magazine for new methods, products, or services which might help me run my business more profitably?

The manager of a business is a busy man. Like Bill Brady, he not only sells, but he buys, advertises, plans promotions, selects and trains people, and does a hundred other things every day. Yet this check list and booklet suggest he also spends considerable time controlling costs. You, as a busy manager, might question whether you have the time.

You cannot escape this careful and close watch over

costs, however, if you are to be successful. The intelligent and sound management of a business is a long, hard job. But the rewards, in the form of greater profits and a feeling of accomplishment, are worth the constant challenge.

TO A MORE PROFITABLE TOMORROW

Can your business afford a system of cost control? Really, there is no alternative. No business can operate for long in a blind condition.

This book has focused on the needs for controlling costs and the techniques of control. It has not attempted to outline a system that would be applicable to every business. This would be impossible because of the wide variation in size, volume, variety of services and locations among businesses of even the same type.

But just as Bill Brady did in Chapter 2, you can find a Jack Larkin who will tailor a system to your present needs and modify it to meet tomorrow's demands.

Cost control can and will work for you. It will help you understand your business as you never have before. Once you have the knack of control, your reward will come in the form of an efficiently managed, tightly controlled operation that will make greater profits for you.

CHAPTER 7

Cost of Doing Business

EXPLANATION:

Following are summaries of the Internal Revenue Service definitions applicable to the IRS data used by Dun & Bradstreet, Inc. as a basis for computing the ratios in this study.

DESCRIPTION OF THE SAMPLE:

"Statistical information was estimated from a sample, selected before audit, of income tax returns filed in the district offices of the Internal Revenue Service and the Office of International Operations."

BUSINESS RECEIPTS (SALES)

"Represent gross receipts, less allowances, rebates, and returns, from the principal business activity. The term reflects income arising out of the sale of goods and services and in some cases other income, such as dividends, interest, rents, and royalties, when such income constitutes the principal business activity. An example of the latter would be rental income in the case of real estate operators or manufacturers who lease instead of sell their product."

In computing the ratios presented business receipts were expressed as the base (100%).

COST OF GOODS SOLD

"Reflects operations involving merchandise as an income-producing factor. It represents the sum of opening inventory, merchandise purchased, labor, and material and supply costs, less closing inventory. In transcribing these data from returns identifiable amounts of such items as taxes paid, depreciation, depletion, amortization, advertising, and contributions under pension plans were excluded from costs of goods sold and transferred to their respective deduction categories."

GROSS MARGIN

"Equals business receipts less cost of goods sold."

SALARIES AND WAGES

"Consists of those salaries and wages not included as a deduction for 'cost of labor' in the cost of goods sold schedule. Salaries to partners, to the taxpayer if a sole proprietor, are not included in this item."

PAYMENTS TO PARTNERS

"This account shows guaranteed payments made to a partner for services or the use of capital where such payments are determined without regard to income of the partnership."

RENT

"Rent paid on business property is deductible as an ordinary and necessary expense. Identifiable amounts of taxes and other expenses paid by lessees in connection with rent paid are included in their respective deduction headings."

INTEREST

"This deduction is permitted for interest paid or accrued in connection with business indebtedness."

TAXES

"State and local taxes paid or accrued on business property or incurred in conducting business are allowable deductions. Also included are Federal import and excise duties and taxes."

BAD DEBTS

"Bad debts may be deducted when there is reasonable certainty that they are uncollectible. A debt which is deducted as uncollectible, if subsequently collected, must be reported as income for the year in which collected."

REPAIRS

"This includes cost of labor and supplies, and other costs necessary for incidental repairs to the property. It does not include capital expenditures which add to the property value, improvements which appreciably prolong its life, or expenditures for restoring or replacing property."

AMORTIZATION, DEPRECIATION AND DEPLETION

"Amortization is the sum of deductions taken in lieu of depreciation for Government-certified emergency facilities for the national defense and the amounts of deferred expenses written off for research and experimental expenditures, exploration and development expenditures, organizational expenditures and trade-mark and trade name expenditures. Depreciation is a deduction of a reasonable allowance for the exhaustion, wear and tear, or obsolescence of property used in a trade or business, or of property held for the production of income. Depletion is deduction from income for a wasting asset such as a mineral deposit, or a stand of timber to recover its cost."

NET PROFIT (OR LOSS) ON BUSINESS RECEIPTS

"On sole proprietorship returns net profit (or loss) represents the difference between business receipts and the sum of cost of goods sold and other business deductions. For partnerships, net profit (or loss) represents the difference between total receipts and sum of cost of goods sold and business deductions. The term net profit is used for both sole proprietorships and partnerships, although in concept the term is not strictly comparable for the two forms of business organization. For example, investment income is reflected in partnership profit but not in sole proprietorship net profit. A further difference is that salaries paid to the owner(s) are a business deduction for a partnership but not for a sole proprietorship."

The following are average operating ratios for 102 lines of business. The ratios represent a percentage of business receipts (sales). All figures were derived from representative samples of the total of all Federal Income Tax returns* filed for the 1962-63 year by proprietorships and partnerships.

COST OF DOING BUSINESS—

INDUSTRY (and total number of returns filed)	Cost of Goods Sold	SELECTED COSTS		
		Merchandise Purchased	Labor	Materials and Supplies
	%	%	%	%
ALL INDUSTRIES (9,182,586)	59.29	42.27	4.44	3.07
RETAIL TRADE (1,514,774)	75.03	69.46	1.55	.94
Apparel and accessories (64,811)	68.29	64.13	1.42	.46
Automotive dealers (65,549)	83.49	68.01	1.59	1.09
Building materials (25,027)	71.01	62.53	3.62	1.96
Drug and proprietary stores (33,918)	68.40	66.36	1.36	.28
Eating and drinking places (298,230)	56.71	50.47	2.57	1.60
Furniture and home furnishings (78,914)	66.89	60.14	2.94	1.25
Gasoline service stations (197,076)	79.54	75.23	1.46	.90
General merchandise (136.359)	74.56	70.96	.71	.86
Grocery stores, meat, fish, fruit and vegetable markets (267,872)	84.47	82.04	.64	.43
Hardware and farm equipment (36,292)	78.36	71.78	1.17	.60
Liquor stores (24,753)	79.69	77.51	1.04	.07
WHOLESALE TRADE (319,131)	75.48	70.11	1.24	1.08
Farm products — raw materials (17,533)	89.00	85.05	.40	.28
Groceries and related products (44,629)	84.56	79.37	.96	.93
Machinery, equipment and supplies (17,911)	64.78	59.83	2.53	1.72
WHOLESALE AND RETAIL TRADES (1,888,602)	75.14	69.61	1.53	.98
MANUFACTURING (180,505)	60.05	36.30	13.57	6.00
Food and kindred products (17,818)	72.53	64.42	3.72	3.14
Lumber and wood products, except furniture (46,656)	49.30	25.59	10.90	3.92
Machinery, except electrical and transportation equipment (16,396)	52.17	17.46	19.56	11.86
Printing, publishing and allied industries (29,523)	47.92	19.23	15.22	7.30
CONSTRUCTION (687,187)	60.78	20.61	13.90	15.99
General trade contractors (116,522)	71.08	17.41	13.12	22.12
Special trade contractors (542,883)	53.80	23.13	14.47	11.68
Electrical work (42,352)	62.86	33.86	13.57	12.22
Plumbing, heating and air conditioning (59,449)	64.45	36.04	12.47	10.36

*Source Book of Statistics of Income, U.S. Treasury Dept. Internal Revenue Service, Statistics Division

PROPRIETORSHIPS

| Gross Margin | SELECTED OPERATING EXPENSES | | | | | | | Profits on Business Receipts |
| | Salaries and Wages | Rent | Interest | Taxes | Bad Debts | Repairs | Depreciation Amortization Depletion | |
%	%	%	%	%	%	%	%	%
40.71	6.46	2.02	1.01	1.67	.15	1.52	4.10	13.39
24.97	6.50	1.89	.38	1.28	.16	.46	1.42	6.11
31.71	7.78	4.08	.41	1.27	.15	.32	1.18	8.16
16.51	4.37	.80	.53	.72	.27	.44	.58	3.18
28.99	6.70	.94	.51	1.51	.53	.47	1.80	7.00
31.60	10.31	2.08	.31	1.58	.09	.32	1.31	10.30
43.29	13.51	3.44	.59	2.61	.05	1.04	2.88	8.30
33.11	7.81	2.30	.57	1.39	.36	.38	1.83	8.37
20.46	6.03	2.05	.18	1.01	.16	.21	.84	4.78
25.44	4.64	1.68	.36	1.31	.14	.45	1.96	7.74
15.53	3.56	1.02	.21	.91	.07	.33	1.04	3.98
21.64	5.70	1.22	.60	1.14	.32	.26	1.15	5.19
20.31	3.98	1.41	.32	1.58	.05	.38	.97	7.50
24.52	3.81	.72	.29	.75	.16	.47	1.39	8.57
11.00	1.28	.19	.31	.34	.02	.49	.97	2.77
15.44	3.53	.41	.16	.38	.08	.37	.92	4.70
35.22	4.51	1.03	.31	.73	.23	.37	1.43	11.00
24.86	6.00	1.64	.36	1.18	.17	.46	1.42	6.55
39.95	8.62	1.32	.64	1.66	.21	1.17	3.37	9.74
27.47	7.12	.67	.36	1.18	.08	.82	1.97	4.81
50.70	10.30	.76	.83	1.75	.08	3.41	5.99	8.57
47.83	9.15	1.58	.62	1.61	.19	.57	4.23	17.43
52.08	12.38	2.18	.82	1.81	.58	.73	4.91	14.32
39.22	7.83	.49	.56	1.25	.14	1.02	2.68	13.56
28.92	5.41	.34	.73	.99	.07	.84	2.05	7.53
46.20	9.36	.59	.43	1.44	.19	1.12	3.05	17.84
37.14	8.19	.63	.36	1.35	.52	.37	1.94	13.82
35.55	7.33	.57	.32	1.40	.23	.39	1.92	13.15

COST OF DOING BUSINESS—

INDUSTRY (and total number of returns filed)	Cost of Goods Sold	SELECTED COSTS		
		Merchandise Purchased	Labor	Materials and Supplies
	%	%	%	%
SERVICES (2,132,751)	19.53	10.13	3.79	3.11
Accounting, auditing and bookkeeping (98,399)	1.78	.07	.80	.33
Automotive (139,145)	53.35	39.36	6.78	4.87
Business (226,871)	32.86	15.22	7.09	3.38
Educational (81,640)	9.30	4.70	.74	1.82
Engineering and architectural (48,424)	14.11	1.84	5.34	1.32
Legal (132,891)	2.81	.09	.74	.31
Lodging services (121,350)	18.14	12.48	1.84	1.70
Hotels (12,728)	29.13	20.79	3.50	2.04
Tourist courts and motels (40,165)	13.24	8.88	1.32	1.23
Medical and other health services (408,685)	6.36	1.67	1.27	2.26
Dentists and dental surgeons (82,898)	8.19	.71	1.68	3.36
Physicians, surgeons and oculists (152,960)	2.75	.54	.50	1.22
Personal services (500,975)	23.54	8.45	7.33	5.05
Beauty and barber shops (298,737)	15.12	2.54	7.05	4.80
Laundries, cleaning and dyeing plants (85,318)	25.28	5.29	10.41	5.21
Recreational (110,695)	21.71	13.89	2.49	1.81
Repair, except automotive (182,279)	43.29	27.43	6.04	7.74
TRANSPORTATION, COMMUNICATION AND SANITARY SERVICES (283,955)	19.67	9.53	3.57	2.00
Motor freight transportation (199,985)	17.22	8.53	3.61	1.53
FINANCE, INSURANCE AND REAL ESTATE (472,674)	20.97	8.22	1.92	2.30
Insurance agents and brokers (168,355)	10.78	2.81	1.34	.32
Real estate agents, brokers and managers (169,375)	10.13	3.68	1.34	.39
Real estate operators, except developers and lessors (51,038)	7.01	2.73	1.04	.53
MINING (34,987)	29.00	4.17	5.03	3.72
AGRICULTURE, FORESTRY AND FISHERIES (3,444,116)	59.33	13.76	7.22	2.19

(L) Loss

PROPRIETORSHIPS, Continued

Gross Margin	SELECTED OPERATING EXPENSES							Profits on Business Receipts
	Salaries and Wages	Rent	Interest	Taxes	Bad Debts	Repairs	Depreciation Amortization Depletion	
%	%	%	%	%	%	%	%	%
80.47	11.84	4.19	.91	1.54	.10	.99	4.82	35.61
98.22	18.78	4.17	.50	1.07	.04	.60	4.26	49.46
46.65	10.07	3.21	.63	1.67	.23	.77	3.11	14.92
67.14	10.51	2.58	.60	1.23	.16	1.00	4.23	24.57
90.70	16.96	4.32	1.11	1.64	.11	1.39	6.10	32.71
85.89	20.55	2.57	.51	1.20	.10	.32	2.81	28.19
97.19	11.08	4.87	.33	.72	.07	.35	2.89	54.06
81.86	10.08	3.67	6.46	5.48	.05	4.35	15.38	7.67
70.87	16.06	7.88	2.57	5.12	.06	3.30	7.66	4.74
86.76	9.45	1.02	8.81	5.68	.05	4.38	19.31	8.92
93.64	10.72	4.02	.49	.98	.03	.52	3.62	54.43
91.81	10.91	4.47	.50	.96	.01	.45	3.35	51.62
97.25	10.58	4.03	.37	.89	.03	.43	3.56	59.36
76.46	15.36	6.15	.84	1.90	.12	1.30	5.84	25.59
84.88	19.88	7.65	.36	1.68	.01	.80	3.34	35.90
74.72	15.46	6.23	1.47	2.27	.12	2.10	9.48	12.67
78.29	13.99	5.12	1.54	2.67	.07	1.96	8.82	9.22
56.71	6.38	2.54	.53	1.37	.22	.78	3.93	25.27
80.33	12.97	1.49	1.17	2.69	.12	6.09	9.75	15.14
82.78	12.35	1.27	1.24	2.95	.11	6.73	10.32	14.58
79.03	7.73	2.16	2.28	1.56	.72	.84	4.87	31.67
89.22	10.23	2.46	.74	.59	.84	.44	3.43	41.20
89.87	6.54	2.48	1.65	1.08	._0	.84	4.96	39.74
92.99	5.05	2.27	12.12	9.99	.60	4.65	21.50	8.10
71.00	9.59	1.47	1.89	2.23	.70	1.85	18.90	6.46(L)
40.67	.73	2.26	3.03	3.32	.01	4.87	10.86	12.23

COST OF DOING BUSINESS—

| INDUSTRY (and total number of returns filed) | Cost of Goods Sold | SELECTED COSTS | | Gross Margin |
| | | Merchandise Purchased | Labor, Supplies | |
	%	%	%	%
ALL INDUSTRIES (932,181)	60.43	47.36	13.11	39.57
RETAIL TRADE (220,585)	73.37	72.12	1.59	26.63
Apparel and accessories (14,547)	66.61	65.60	1.29	33.39
Automotive dealers (15,612)	83.36	80.58	3.51	16.64
Building materials (5,301)	72.37	69.83	2.46	27.63
Drug and proprietary stores (7,888)	66.28	66.94	.31	33.72
Eating and drinking places (42,112)	49.92	48.23	1.51	50.08
Furniture and home furnishings (14,461)	64.98	64.30	1.76	35.02
Gasoline service stations (29,257)	76.69	74.86	1.74	23.31
General merchandise (11,584)	73.56	73.60	.83	26.44
Grocery stores, meat, fish, fruit and vegetable markets (33,283)	81.62	80.88	.65	18.38
Hardware and farm equipment (9,830)	77.35	77.11	1.09	22.65
Liquor stores (5,612)	78.46	78.33	.53	21.54
WHOLESALE TRADE (40,960)	82.02	79.77	2.22	17.98
Farm products — raw materials (3,480)	92.02	88.79	2.65	7.98
Groceries and related products (7,383)	85.19	82.70	2.34	14.81
Machinery, equipment and supplies (3,095)	73.12	72.37	2.01	26.88
WHOLESALE AND RETAIL TRADES (267,493)	76.33	74.72	1.82	23.67
MANUFACTURING (43,091)	73.19	45.61	27.66	26.81
Apparel and other finished products (3,334)	77.95	39.53	38.76	22.05
Food and kindred products (5,061)	81.44	64.11	17.22	18.56
Lumber and wood products, except furniture (7,258)	73.03	37.51	36.09	26.97
Machinery, except electrical and transportation equipment (5,275)	63.74	30.80	33.54	36.26
Printing, publishing and allied trades (6,429)	59.30	26.12	33.31	40.70
CONSTRUCTION (58,164)	77.66	21.98	55.07	22.34
General trade contractors (18,949)	83.05	16.93	65.25	16.95
Special trade contractors (36,279)	69.07	30.75	38.20	30.93

(L) Loss

PARTNERSHIPS

SELECTED OPERATING EXPENSES								Profits on Business Receipts
Salaries and Wages	Payments to Partners	Rent	Interest	Taxes	Bad Debts	Repairs	Depreciation Amortization Depletion	
%	%	%	%	%	%	%	%	%
8.38	1.53	1.82	1.50	2.14	.18	.92	4.71	11.77
8.21	1.31	1.78	.35	1.47	.18	.37	1.16	6.73
9.71	1.84	3.80	.36	1.45	.21	.25	.99	8.40
5.44	.94	.75	.42	.69	.27	.25	.51	3.90
10.10	1.58	.69	.53	1.80	.41	.38	1.38	6.43
9.99	2.38	2.13	.20	1.71	.15	.28	1.09	11.07
17.99	1.56	3.51	.55	3.18	.04	1.12	2.75	10.23
10.15	1.89	2.27	.55	1.56	.45	.30	1.14	8.71
6.47	1.14	2.07	.19	1.28	.14	.19	.82	6.81
7.68	1.36	1.68	.36	1.54	.12	.31	1.53	6.42
5.49	.71	1.05	.19	1.12	.04	.30	.93	4.76
6.96	1.54	1.00	.42	1.36	.27	.19	.91	5.92
4.58	.94	1.77	.30	1.87	.12	.32	.97	7.58
5.55	.78	.62	.29	.87	.17	.22	.75	4.63
2.03	.27	.17	.35	.26	.05	.19	.60	1.80
5.21	.59	.47	.15	.51	.12	.20	.58	3.31
8.27	1.71	.78	.44	.97	.30	.26	1.09	7.75
7.30	1.13	1.37	.33	1.28	.18	.32	1.02	6.01
1.95	1.60	1.05	.42	1.73	.19	.78	2.29	8.94
2.30	1.05	1.43	.34	1.98	.20	.23	.69	6.65
1.81	.82	.54	.35	1.01	.09	.72	1.79	5.07
1.08	1.23	.61	.77	2.08	.20	2.16	4.76	6.16
1.95	2.86	1.21	.41	2.04	.27	.51	3.11	16.05
3.18	3.24	2.14	.42	1.90	.23	.67	2.84	15.47
1.38	1.44	.36	.50	1.37	.10	.74	2.31	8.73
1.15	.86	.30	.59	1.08	.05	.68	2.26	5.63
1.68	2.42	.47	.36	1.85	.14	.81	2.28	13.63

84

COST OF DOING BUSINESS—

INDUSTRY (and total number of returns filed)	Cost of Goods Sold	SELECTED COSTS		Gross Margin
		Merchan- dise Pur- chased	Labor, Sup- plies	
	%	%	%	%
SERVICES (166,737)	14.07	7.85	6.13	85.93
Accounting, auditing and bookkeeping (8,534)	1.24	.19	1.05	98.76
Automotive (16,932)	49.78	38.25	11.37	50.22
Business (18,348)	31.37	15.06	15.70	68.63
Engineering and architectural (6,325)	13.89	1.54	12.16	86.11
Legal (21,418)	2.17	.25	1.86	97.83
Lodging (14,422)	17.41	11.75	5.59	82.59
Medical and other health services (20,071)	4.10	1.90	2.07	95.90
Physicians, surgeons and oculists (10,457)	1.08	.57	.50	98.92
Personal services (34,630)	22.02	10.72	11.23	77.98
Laundries, cleaning and dyeing plants (14,511)	21.78	6.60	15.14	78.22
Recreational (14,142)	17.84	10.45	7.46	82.16
Repair, except automotive (9,443)	43.82	35.53	8.83	56.18
TRANSPORTATION, COMMUNICATION AND SANITARY SERVICES (17,032)	54.83	18.11	36.71	45.17
Motor freight transportation (11,364)	52.35	14.58	37.74	47.65
FINANCE, INSURANCE AND REAL ESTATE (229,400)	4.45	1.96	2.22	95.55
Insurance agents and brokers (12,735)	19.17	8.68	9.53	80.83
Real estate operators, except developers and lessors (149,244)	.24	.05	.15	99.76
Security and commodity brokers and dealers (4,077)	.15	.06	.12	99.85
MINING (15,040)	54.87	6.37	47.90	45.13
AGRICULTURE, FORESTRY AND FISHERIES (133,647)	57.89	24.63	33.56	42.11

(L) Loss

PARTNERSHIPS, Continued

SELECTED OPERATING EXPENSES								Profits on Business Receipts
Salaries and Wages	Payments to Partners	Rent	Interest	Taxes	Bad Debts	Repairs	Depreciation Amortization Depletion	Profits on Business Receipts
%	%	%	%	%	%	%	%	%
21.59	2.63	4.24	.87	2.03	.12	.81	4.14	32.69
42.36	5.10	3.08	.28	1.80	.10	.15	1.29	30.68
10.32	2.60	4.13	.77	2.00	.30	.77	3.57	15.18
16.76	2.58	2.57	.99	1.84	.18	.99	5.45	20.01
31.51	3.24	2.62	.32	1.67	.07	.14	.96	23.51
20.09	2.16	4.83	.16	1.16	.05	.19	1.18	53.96
18.50	1.30	6.72	5.67	6.49	.19	3.73	14.45	5.55
19.07	1.94	4.67	.38	1.42	.05	.42	1.70	51.02
14.79	1.33	4.39	.20	1.08	.01	.27	1.29	62.29
19.88	2.75	4.52	.90	2.43	.19	1.65	6.21	19.19
22.67	2.22	4.65	1.14	2.82	.07	2.17	7.92	10.70
16.90	2.05	4.97	2.03	3.31	.07	1.66	17.24	6.07
9.86	4.03	2.17	.38	1.69	.26	.70	2.80	21.57
2.13	2.26	1.43	.89	3.41	.21	3.25	6.64	12.48
2.21	2.36	1.56	.97	4.13	.17	3.75	7.27	12.30
16.12	2.70	2.73	13.77	9.60	.48	2.65	14.51	19.14
18.24	4.53	2.29	.53	1.21	.84	.19	1.47	30.88
4.57	.45	2.44	18.75	15.66	.27	4.89	26.00	9.45
44.38	6.45	4.22	9.89	3.81	.19	.26	1.23	13.69
1.58	1.42	.69	1.21	2.92	.20	2.83	18.30	.41(L)
1.65	.91	2.53	2.08	2.51	.04	3.41	6.73	13.14

The following operating ratios for 185 lines of business have been derived to provide a guide as to the average amount spent by corporations for these items. They represent a percentage of business receipts as reported by a representative sample of the total of all Federal Income Tax returns* filed for 1962-1963.

COST OF DOING BUSINESS RATIOS—

Industry (and total number of returns filed)	Cost of Goods Sold	Gross Margin	SELECTED OPERATING EXPENSES Compen- sation of officers
	%	%	%
AI.L INDUSTRIAL GROUPS (1,268,042)	71.27	28.73	1.89
CONSTRUCTION (90,604)	83.99	16.01	3.34
General building contractors (33,151)	89.08	10.92	2.69
Highway & Street construction & heavy construction (9,801)	82.76	17.24	2.29
Special trade contractors (46,132)	79.62	20.38	4.70
Real estate operators (except developers) & lessors of buildings (171,430)	—	—	2.87
Subdividers & developers & operative builders (46,576)	—	—	11.46
WHOLESALERS & RETAILERS (388,852)	79.65	20.35	1.78
RETAILERS (245,187)	74.14	25.86	1.89
Food (18,085)	79.48	20.52	.62
General Merchandise (15,814)	64.87	35.13	.73
Department stores (4,146)	65.18	34.82	.49
Mail order houses (1,096)	55.64	44.36	1.31
Limited price variety stores (2,557)	62.70	37.30	.61
Merchandise vending machine operators, direct selling organiz. & other general mdse. stores (8,015)	69.13	30.87	2.43
Apparel & accessories (29,128)	65.80	34.20	2.98
Furniture, home furnishings & equipment (23,332)	66.38	33.62	4.38
Automotive dealers & gasoline service stations (41,602)	85.45	14.55	1.67
Motor vehicle dealers (25,822)	86.95	13.05	1.50
Tire, battery & accessory dealers, miscellaneous aircraft, marine & automotive dealers (8,622)	74.29	25.71	3.36
Gasoline service stations (7,158)	76.57	23.43	2.14
Eating & drinking places (38,178)	48.67	51.33	4.16
Building materials (16,951)	76.01	23.99	3.29

*Source Book of Statistics of Income, U.S. Treasury Dept. Internal Revenue Service, Statistics Division
†Excludes Federal Income Taxes   —Not computed

CORPORATIONS

SELECTED OPERATING EXPENSES							
Rent paid on Business Property	Repairs	Bad Debts	Interest Paid	Taxes Paid+	Amortization Depreciation Depletion	Advertising	Pension & Other Employee Benefit Plans
%	%	%	%	%	%	%	%
1.24	.87	.39	2.05	2.77	3.57	1.16	.92
.55	.55	.21	.57	1.61	1.85	.23	.48
.32	.23	.16	.70	1.05	.98	.26	.26
.69	1.27	.18	.67	1.68	3.90	.10	.44
.69	.39	.28	.36	2.14	1.36	.30	.74
4.76	3.84	.31	17.25	15.33	19.87	.44	.16
1.15	1.51	.72	13.79	5.82	4.58	4.10	.35
1.34	.26	.22	.40	1.17	.85	1.05	.25
2.09	.35	.23	.41	1.38	1.10	1.54	.29
1.45	.28	.03	.15	.95	1.02	1.32	.40
2.52	.38	.34	.54	1.86	1.50	2.57	.46
2.11	.37	.31	.49	1.93	1.31	2.62	.55
1.20	.22	1.95	1.45	1.13	.63	9.27	.37
5.21	.37	.09	.51	1.80	2.04	1.19	.23
2.58	.44	.25	.56	1.78	2.52	1.22	.15
5.35	.33	.22	.40	1.66	1.03	2.30	.22
2.94	.34	.68	.71	1.60	.89	3.04	.19
.92	.24	.17	.44	.86	.52	.86	.09
.70	.21	.15	.40	.65	.39	.82	.09
2.66	.47	.39	.86	1.29	1.38	1.36	.11
2.05	.42	.20	.46	3.42	1.52	.79	.09
4.99	1.14	.07	.52	3.07	2.86	1.02	.40
.77	.40	.55	.60	1.58	1.15	.85	.23

COST OF DOING BUSINESS RATIOS—

Industry (and total number of returns filed)	Cost of Goods Sold	Gross Margin	SELECTED OPERATING EXPENSES Compen-sation of officers
RETAILERS, Continued	%	%	%
Hardware & farm equipment (10,499)	77.79	22.21	3.69
Drug stores & proprietary stores (12,423)	68.29	31.71	3.68
Liquor stores (6,132)	80.63	19.37	4.02
Jewelry stores (4,529)	57.26	42.74	4.85
WHOLESALERS (132,372)	85.32	14.68	1.64
Groceries & related products (16,099)	89.93	10.07	1.02
Meats & meat products (2,382)	90.51	9.49	1.07
Poultry & poultry products, fish & sea foods, & other groceries & related products (13,717)	89.84	10.16	1.01
Electrical goods, hardware & plumbing & heating equipment & supplies (14,585)	81.65	18.35	2.08
Electrical goods (7,099)	82.84	17.16	1.81
Hardware & plumbing & heating equip. & supplies (7,486)	80.17	19.83	2.41
Beer, wine, distilled alcoholic beverages (3,201)	84.66	15.34	.96
Dry goods & apparel (8,510)	83.21	16.79	2.43
Drugs, chemicals & allied products (5,915)	79.50	20.50	1.36
Lumber & construction materials (7,725)	85.41	14.59	1.99
Machinery, equipment & supplies (17,022)	78.33	21.67	3.03
Motor vehicles & automotive equipment (7,685)	82.85	17.15	1.75
Farm products—raw materials (5,332)	94.23	5.77	.56
MANUFACTURING (183,149)	70.99	29.01	1.26
Beverage Industries (3,207)	56.71	43.29	.91
Bottled & canned soft drinks & carbonated waters & flavoring extracts & flavoring sirups (2,771)	52.35	47.65	2.15
Malt liquors and malt (166)	43.44	56.56	.51
Distilled, rectified & blended liquors (143)	73.01	26.99	.29
Food and kindred products (16,796)	79.73	20.27	.76
Meat products (2,448)	90.21	9.79	.43
Dairy products (3,815)	79.17	20.83	.86
Canning & preserving fruits, vegs. & sea foods (2,150)	76.22	23.78	.93
Grain mill products (2,256)	79.99	20.01	.71
Bakery products (2,777)	62.11	37.89	1.27

†Excludes Federal Income Taxes

CORPORATIONS, Continued

SELECTED OPERATING EXPENSES

Rent paid on Business Property	Repairs	Bad Debts	Interest Paid	Taxes Paid†	Amortization Depreciation Depletion	Advertising	Pension & Other Employee Benefit Plans
%	%	%	%	%	%	%	%
1.60	.25	.37	.60	1.34	.86	.88	.14
3.15	.33	.09	.28	1.57	1.11	1.37	.28
2.07	.23	.05	.36	1.80	.94	.57	.07
4.59	.41	1.28	.82	2.34	.99	4.13	.28
.57	.17	.21	.38	.96	.57	.56	.21
.41	.17	.12	.22	.53	.48	.30	.14
.35	.15	.13	.17	.49	.33	.13	.10
.42	.17	.12	.22	.54	.50	.33	.15
.65	.10	.34	.36	.83	.42	.79	.27
.62	.07	.32	.33	.68	.33	1.18	.25
.70	.14	.37	.40	1.02	.54	.30	.29
.45	.10	.10	.25	3.25	.29	1.21	.23
.70	.05	.18	.57	1.25	.24	.48	.20
.44	.10	.12	.22	.70	.47	1.98	.30
.57	.23	.46	.44	.79	.73	.27	.18
.74	.20	.35	.57	.92	.87	.52	.31
.72	.09	.18	.25	.77	.42	.74	.17
.29	.23	.05	.61	.39	.59	.08	.07
.74	1.36	.15	.62	2.93	3.76	1.41	1.25
.48	.76	.08	.60	15.99	2.89	4.99	.77
.99	1.18	.16	.58	3.17	4.38	6.16	.66
.34	1.05	.09	.33	28.02	3.04	6.89	1.23
.19	.21	.02	.84	13.80	1.62	2.18	.43
.51	.82	.11	.39	1.29	1.69	2.02	.63
.28	.55	.05	.20	.64	.83	.56	.47
.68	.93	.18	.29	1.26	2.16	1.57	.69
.59	1.08	.09	.94	1.74	1.98	2.72	.53
.26	.82	.19	.50	.88	1.69	3.18	.39
1.06	1.11	.12	.30	2.06	2.55	2.48	1.41

COST OF DOING BUSINESS RATIOS—

Industry (and total number of returns filed)	Cost of Goods Sold	Gross Margin	SELECTED OPERATING EXPENSES Compensation of officers
MANUFACTURING, Continued	%	%	%
Sugar (156)	76.10	23.90	.37
Confectionery & related products (774)	65.85	34.15	1.42
Veg. oil mills & animal, marine & edible fats & oils (527)	86.55	13.45	.72
Tobacco manufacturers (187)	58.00	42.00	.24
Textile mill products (6,202)	80.22	19.78	1.34
Yarn & thread mills (437)	82.38	17.62	1.03
Broad woven fabric mills, cotton (372)	81.19	18.81	.62
Broad woven fabric mills, man-made fiber & silk (116)	80.76	19.24	.64
Broad woven fabric mills, wool: including dyeing & finishing (300)	83.08	16.92	1.04
Narrow fabrics & other smallwares mills: cotton, wool, silk & man-made fiber (559)	76.54	23.46	3.23
Knitting mills (1,967)	77.64	22.36	1.92
Dyeing & finishing textiles, except wool fabrics & knit goods (795)	81.08	18.92	2.39
Floor covering mills (276)	79.17	20.83	1.19
Apparel & other finished products made from fabrics & similar materials (17,684)	78.56	21.44	2.61
Men's, youths', & boys' suits, coats, overcoats, furnishings, work clothing & allied garments (3,137)	79.23	20.77	1.93
Women's, misses', children's & infants' outerwear & undergarments (8,727)	77.96	22.04	2.68
Hats, caps & millinery, fur goods & other apparel & accessories (2,253)	78.35	21.65	3.79
Lumber & wood products, except furniture (9,178)	77.40	22.60	1.98
Logging camps, logging contractors, & sawmills & planing mills (3,505)	76.51	23.49	1.43
Millwork, veneer plywood & prefabricated structural wood products (3,376)	78.34	21.66	2.08
Wooden containers & other wood products (2,297)	77.45	22.55	3.24
Furniture & fixtures (5,986)	73.36	26.64	2.79
Household furniture (3,791)	74.63	25.37	2.74
Office, public bldg. & other furniture & fixtures (2,195)	71.12	28.88	2.88
Paper & allied products (3,581)	69.08	30.92	1.24
Pulp mills (31)	70.30	29.70	.62
Paper, paperboard, building paper & building board mills (351)	68.71	31.29	.55

†Excludes Federal Income Taxes

CORPORATIONS, Continued

SELECTED OPERATING EXPENSES

Rent paid on Business Property	Repairs	Bad Debts	Interest Paid	Taxes Paid†	Amortization Depreciation Depletion	Advertising	Pension & Other Employee Benefit Plans
%	%	%	%	%	%	%	%
.41	2.05	.02	.62	5.80	2.79	.28	.88
.99	.79	.16	.26	1.75	1.85	4.22	.96
.45	.88	.19	.82	.94	1.92	.57	.24
.11	.25	.01	.62	18.35	.91	5.28	.88
.72	.85	.10	.69	1.83	2.57	.59	.53
.38	.68	.12	.49	1.70	2.75	.36	.44
.31	1.25	.05	.57	1.87	3.30	.52	.52
.80	.19	.04	.89	1.66	2.72	.40	.46
.65	.80	.13	1.00	1.91	2.32	.32	.54
1.04	.46	.07	.55	2.02	2.07	.36	.68
.86	.49	.08	.65	2.00	2.45	1.07	.56
1.35	.91	.10	.56	1.85	1.89	.23	.76
.98	.58	.15	.61	1.47	2.24	1.18	.18
1.10	.20	.17	.48	1.88	.72	.89	.63
.94	.19	.16	.63	2.03	.73	.97	.62
1.12	.16	.19	.34	1.80	.59	.96	.71
1.38	.23	.15	.72	1.86	.68	.78	.58
.63	.84	.33	1.00	2.36	5.54	.41	.40
.45	.81	.27	1.05	2.80	8.33	.24	.35
.76	.93	.37	1.14	1.95	3.84	.59	.43
.81	.72	.42	.55	2.14	2.20	.40	.47
1.17	.56	.31	.47	2.13	1.58	1.17	.78
1.11	.54	.31	.46	2.10	1.45	1.25	.64
1.27	.61	.29	.50	2.18	1.80	1.02	1.03
.76	2.15	.10	.82	2.22	5.07	.80	1.04
.17	4.36	.02	3.71	2.35	8.11	.61	1.15
.53	2.69	.06	.87	2.40	6.49	.88	1.19

COST OF DOING BUSINESS RATIOS—

Industry (and total number of returns filed)	Cost of Goods Sold	Gross Margin	SELECTED OPERATING EXPENSES Compen- sation of officers
MANUFACTURING, Continued	%	%	%
Paperboard containers & boxes (1,503)	71.11	28.89	2.20
Converted paper & paperboard products, except containers & boxes (1,696)	68.28	31.72	2.22
Printing, publishing & allied industries (21,698)	65.48	34.52	3.35
Newspapers: publishing, publishing & printing (4,050)	65.32	34.68	2.16
Periodicals: publishing, publishing & printing (1,733)	69.56	30.44	2.18
Books (1,260)	55.74	44.26	2.63
Commercial printing, manifold business forms, & greeting cards (9,718)	67.39	32.61	4.52
Chemicals & allied products (11,032)	59.15	40.85	1.11
Industrial inorganic and organic chemicals (1,430)	65.40	34.60	1.15
Plastics materials & synthetic resins & rubber, synthetic & other man-made fibers, except glass (1,226)	58.11	41.89	.71
Drugs (1,738)	40.79	59.21	1.48
Soap, detergents & cleaning preparations (1,456)	65.25	34.75	1.26
Paints, varnishes, lacquers, enamels & allied prod. (1,730)	68.53	31.47	1.95
Perfumes, cosmetics & other toilet preparations (766)	44.53	55.47	1.74
Agricultural chemicals (1,115)	75.44	24.56	1.37
Gum & wood chemicals & other chemical products (1,372)	58.17	41.83	1.48
Petroleum refining (335)	70.02	29.98	.14
Paving & roofing materials & other products of petroleum and coal (723)	71.70	28.30	1.88
Rubber & miscellaneous plastics products (4,754)	68.75	31.25	1.46
Tires & inner tubes (86)	67.70	32.30	.18
Rubber footwear, reclaimed rubber & other fabricated rubber products (1,137)	67.45	32.55	1.89
Leather & leather products (2,590)	78.38	21.62	1.97
Footwear, except rubber (845)	78.39	21.61	1.50
Stone, clay & glass products (8,358)	65.84	34.16	1.76
Flat glass, glass & glassware, pressed or blown & glass products made of purchased glass (832)	64.68	35.32	1.02
Cement, hydraulic (100)	49.23	50.77	.96
Structural clay products (654)	65.80	34.20	2.48
Pottery & related products (417)	68.97	31.03	2.42
Concrete, gypsum & plaster products (4,909)	66.68	33.32	2.60

†Excludes Federal Income Taxes

CORPORATIONS, Continued

SELECTED OPERATING EXPENSES

Rent paid on Business Property	Repairs	Bad Debts	Interest Paid	Taxes Paid†	Amortization Depreciation Depletion	Advertising	Pension & Other Employee Benefit Plans
%	%	%	%	%	%	%	%
1.44	1.69	.18	.46	1.96	2.94	.24	.93
.88	.93	.16	.58	1.96	2.92	1.07	.75
1.15	.48	.39	.59	2.13	2.58	1.09	1.12
.66	.47	.46	.53	2.46	2.83	.42	1.38
1.25	.34	.21	.46	1.29	1.59	1.88	.97
1.15	.28	.78	.92	1.61	1.55	3.62	.90
1.40	.57	.31	.58	2.30	3.03	.56	1.07
.68	1.58	.14	.71	1.77	5.66	3.99	1.49
.73	1.97	.09	1.20	1.77	6.85	1.16	1.34
.50	1.74	.08	.66	1.89	8.39	1.30	2.29
.72	.80	.13	.35	2.04	2.99	10.51	1.53
.39	1.04	.06	.31	1.00	1.83	7.98	1.01
.91	.79	.34	.32	1.51	2.25	1.65	.93
1.04	.36	.28	.33	1.65	1.17	14.72	.86
.50	1.57	.26	1.03	1.54	4.72	.72	.55
1.00	1.92	.09	.55	1.98	6.21	1.62	1.39
1.34	1.49	.10	.60	3.98	8.92	.49	1.07
.70	1.91	.63	1.11	1.79	3.47	.85	.89
1.03	1.42	.23	.62	3.73	3.23	1.62	1.24
.87	1.85	.22	.65	4.96	3.71	2.09	1.58
.98	1.10	.16	.60	2.88	2.49	1.56	1.15
.86	.45	.17	.59	2.12	1.06	1.19	.85
.81	.36	.17	.67	2.31	1.00	1.43	.89
.68	2.74	.27	.72	2.48	5.81	.78	1.17
.78	3.85	.17	.39	2.54	4.60	1.01	1.51
.41	3.97	.16	1.50	3.12	14.67	0.37	1.74
.41	2.14	.26	.93	3.07	6.09	.74	1.28
.75	1.00	.22	.62	3.22	2.28	1.64	1.04
.82	2.30	.51	.92	2.24	5.75	.59	.58

COST OF DOING BUSINESS RATIOS—

Industry (and total number of returns filed)	Cost of Goods Sold	Gross Margin	SELECTED OPERATING EXPENSES Compensation of officers
MANUFACTURING, Continued	%	%	%
Cut stone & stone products & abrasive, asbestos, & other nonmetallic mineral products (1,446)	72.44	27.56	1.45
Primary metal industries (4,637)	72.91	27.09	.78
Blast furnaces, steel works & rolling & finishing mills (303)	70.97	29.03	.29
Iron & steel foundries (1,077)	73.01	26.99	2.09
Primary & secondary smelting & refining, & rolling, drawing, & extruding of nonferrous metals & alloys (900)	75.19	24.81	.61
Nonferrous foundries (1,339)	74.77	25.23	3.70
Fabricated metal products (including ordnance) except machinery & transportation equipment (18,993)	72.74	27.26	2.39
Metal cans (85)	70.78	29.22	.29
Cutlery, hand tools & general hardware (1,081)	61.14	38.86	2.31
Heating apparatus (except electric) & plumbing fixt. (836)	72.68	27.32	1.17
Fabricated structural metal products (5,383)	77.18	22.82	2.82
Screw machine products, & bolts, nuts, screws, rivets & washers (1,662)	70.19	29.81	3.15
Metal stampings (1,682)	73.74	26.26	2.71
Coating, engraving & allied services (2,753)	66.50	33.50	6.96
Machinery, except electrical & transportation equip. (19,458)	66.39	33.61	2.02
Engines & turbines (185)	71.22	28.78	.93
Farm machinery & equipment (829)	72.41	27.59	.68
Construction, mining, & materials handling machinery & equipment (1,774)	70.96	29.04	1.44
Metalworking machinery & equipment (4,653)	67.30	32.70	3.60
Special industry machinery, except metalworking machinery (3,024)	69.18	30.82	2.71
General industrial machinery & equipment (1,894)	66.35	33.65	2.05
Office, computing, & accounting machines (313)	47.24	52.76	.50
Service industry machines (966)	73.43	26.57	2.08
Electrical machinery, equipment & supplies (8,133)	68.62	31.38	1.11
Electrical transmission & distribution equip. (717)	67.60	32.40	.49
Electric industrial apparatus (850)	68.10	31.90	1.71
Household appliances (397)	65.24	34.76	.81
Electric lighting & wiring equipment (1,252)	70.16	29.84	2.51

†Excludes Federal Income Taxes

CORPORATIONS, Continued

SELECTED OPERATING EXPENSES

Rent paid on Business Property	Repairs	Bad Debts	Interest Paid	Taxes Paid†	Amortization Depreciation Depletion	Advertising	Pension & Other Employee Benefit Plans
%	%	%	%	%	%	%	%
.59	2.02	.13	.45	2.15	4.03	.81	1.31
.39	4.72	.09	1.09	2.37	5.86	.38	1.97
.35	6.97	.05	1.25	2.67	7.00	.30	2.50
.32	2.73	.16	.42	2.88	3.56	.30	1.96
.41	2.20	.14	1.15	1.82	5.44	.59	1.32
.64	1.00	.16	.54	2.33	2.29	.37	1.05
.86	1.23	.21	.58	2.13	2.77	.86	1.14
.96	3.15	.11	.94	2.21	5.17	.79	1.56
.63	1.38	.20	.42	2.50	2.72	3.28	1.43
.66	1.18	.24	.47	2.13	2.47	1.06	1.10
.81	.60	.37	.66	1.98	1.92	.59	.84
.80	1.15	.13	.48	2.26	3.19	.50	1.22
.78	1.66	.19	.56	2.34	2.97	.58	1.12
1.86	1.10	.36	.41	2.61	2.81	.62	.92
.72	1.21	.19	.73	2.43	3.82	.96	1.57
.37	1.94	.13	.42	2.00	2.69	1.41	2.00
.51	2.44	.19	1.02	2.29	3.15	1.05	2.16
.59	1.37	.19	.70	2.17	2.75	.84	1.40
.73	1.27	.13	.51	2.71	3.31	.90	1.77
.79	.83	.28	.67	2.27	3.00	.93	1.48
.59	1.09	.14	.43	2.26	2.78	1.09	1.68
.99	.42	.13	.96	3.28	9.50	.71	1.49
.65	.71	.32	.97	1.80	2.05	1.44	.94
.75	.79	.15	.62	2.82	2.50	1.44	1.47
.21	.19	.07	.28	2.48	2.92	1.59	1.89
.57	1.02	.10	.29	2.44	2.36	1.13	1.84
.91	.93	.36	.94	2.22	2.46	2.48	1.06
1.11	.69	.13	.43	2.08	1.81	1.03	1.00

COST OF DOING BUSINESS RATIOS—

Industry (and total number of returns filed)	Cost of Goods Sold	Gross Margin	SELECTED OPERATING EXPENSES Compen-sation of officers
MANUFACTURING, Continued	%	%	%
Radio & television receiving sets, except communcation types (616)	70.52	29.48	.52
Communication equipment (686)	75.84	24.16	1.13
Electronic components & accessories (2,630)	71.77	28.23	2.53
Transportation equipment except motor vehicles (2,357)	81.54	18.46	.46
Aircraft (187)	82.44	17.56	.15
Aircraft parts (609)	79.73	20.27	.66
Ship & Boat building & repairing (979)	84.11	15.89	1.33
Railroad equipment (94)	76.87	23.13	.77
Motorcycles, bicycles, & parts & other transportation equipment (488)	84.04	15.96	1.42
Motor vehicles, passenger car bodies, truck & bus bodies & truck trailers (810)	68.21	31.79	.19
Motor vehicle parts & accessories (1,432)	72.81	27.19	1.40
Professional, scientific & controlling instruments; photographic & optical goods; watches & clocks (4,267)	61.09	38.91	1.75
Engineering, lab., scientific & research, & measuring & controlling instruments & associated equipment (1,725)	66.13	33.87	1.42
Optical instruments & lenses, surgical, medical & dental instruments & suppl. & ophthalmic goods (1,901)	58.19	41.81	3.31
Photographic equipment & supplies (456)	51.02	48.98	1.07
Watches, clocks, clockwork operated devices & parts (185)	67.46	32.54	1.86
Jewelry, silverware & plated ware (1,472)	67.39	32.61	4.28
Costume jewelry & costume novelties, except precious metal (622)	69.54	30.46	6.33
Toys, amusement, sporting & athletic goods (1,746)	68.79	31.21	2.24
SERVICE, TRANSPORTATION & COMMUNICATION			
Security & commodity brokers, dealers, exchanges & services (4,183)	—	—	13.72
Insurance agents, brokers & service (21,385)	—	—	16.42
Hotels, rooming houses, camps & other lodging places (15,014)	46.49	53.51	2.51
Laundries, laundry services & cleaning & dyeing plants (14,416)	53.22	46.78	4.85
Photographic studios, including commercial photography (1,867)	51.87	48.13	8.11
Beauty & barber shops, shoe repair & pressing shops, funeral services & other personal services (9,280)	41.85	58.15	11.90

†Excludes Federal Income Taxes　　　　—Not computed

CORPORATIONS, Continued

SELECTED OPERATING EXPENSES

Rent paid on Business Property	Repairs	Bad Debts	Interest Paid	Taxes Paid†	Amortiza- tion Deprecia- tion Depletion	Adver- tising	Pension & Other Employee Benefit Plans
%	%	%	%	%	%	%	%
.55	.79	.23	.74	4.49	2.56	1.77	1.34
1.19	.91	.09	1.03	2.32	1.93	.52	1.41
1.27	.79	.18	.89	2.75	2.48	.86	.98
.75	1.15	.04	.56	2.17	1.89	.23	1.55
.73	.91	.01	.54	2.11	1.43	.15	1.57
.90	1.49	.05	.49	2.40	2.14	.24	1.80
.75	1.11	.09	.60	2.40	2.06	.48	.90
.51	2.29	.07	1.18	2.05	5.17	.36	1.75
.42	.44	.24	.39	1.40	1.18	.67	.42
.14	1.00	.02	.25	3.73	3.08	.74	2.61
.49	1.65	.10	.32	2.56	2.68	.71	1.73
1.03	.96	.13	.66	2.57	3.41	2.31	2.08
1.08	.75	.12	.84	2.18	3.30	1.23	1.95
1.23	.94	.13	.50	2.25	2.30	3.36	1.15
.81	1.49	.12	.37	3.59	4.95	3.11	3.33
.78	.85	.28	.84	3.12	1.99	5.45	.72
.93	.73	.44	.64	2.23	1.33	2.06	.72
1.79	.35	.32	.43	2.19	1.23	1.19	.49
1.07	.42	1.07	2.22	2.75	1.92	3.42	.62
3.49	.18	.20	9.29	3.13	1.15	1.56	2.00
3.42	.24	.53	.59	1.98	1.65	1.08	1.24
7.57	3.17	.42	5.22	6.43	9.82	2.57	.53
3.55	1.51	.19	.93	3.39	5.35	1.19	.57
3.36	.58	.32	.59	2.09	2.57	2.21	.46
5.55	1.17	.62	.98	3.18	4.60	2.86	.42

COST OF DOING BUSINESS RATIOS—

Industry (and total number of returns filed) SERVICE, TRANSPORTATION & COMMUNICATION, Continued	Cost of Goods Sold %	Gross Margin %	SELECTED OPERATING EXPENSES Compensation of officers %
Advertising (6,578)	73.90	26.10	5.08
Automobile repair, automobile services & garages (15,329)	45.33	54.67	4.71
Motion picture production & distribution & motion picture service industries (3,224)	71.84	28.16	2.24
Motion picture theaters (4,201)	51.65	48.35	3.37
Railroad transportation (474)	69.47	30.53	.29
Local & suburban transit (922)	67.72	32.28	2.03
Motor freight transportation & warehousing (20,769)	67.54	32.46	2.97
Taxicabs, intercity passenger transportation, school buses & other local & interurban passenger trans. (6,654)	64.52	35.48	2.58
Pipeline transportation (290)	57.37	42.63	.29
Water transportation (4,181)	72.21	27.79	1.56
Transportation by air (1,662)	67.88	32.12	.66
Telephone communication (wire or radio) (2,466)	51.31	48.69	.21
Telegraph communication (wire & radio) (43)	66.29	33.71	.33
Radio broadcasting & television (3,593)	57.19	42.81	2.48
Electric companies & systems & combination companies & systems (455)	39.90	60.10	.37
Gas companies & systems (1,496)	61.49	38.51	.43
Water supply & other sanitary services (4,352)	45.89	54.11	3.70
AGRICULTURE & MINING			
Agriculture, forestry & fisheries (22,130)	72.38	27.62	2.80
Mining (13,539)	60.31	39.69	1.44
Metal mining (1,154)	54.95	45.05	.48
Bituminous coal & lignite mining (2,205)	70.06	29.94	1.32
Crude petroleum & natural gas (6,592)	57.71	42.29	1.31
Mining & quarrying of nonmetallic minerals & anthracite mining (3,588)	63.89	36.11	2.67
Dimension stone, crushed & broken stone & sand & gravel (2,706)	60.44	39.56	3.26

†Excludes Federal Income Taxes   —Not computed

CORPORATIONS, Continued

SELECTED OPERATING EXPENSES

Rent paid on Business Property %	Repairs %	Bad Debts %	Interest Paid %	Taxes Paid† %	Amortization Depreciation Depletion %	Advertising %	Pension & Other Employee Benefit Plans %
1.62	.19	.15	.20	.93	1.04	.70	.93
6.82	1.54	.65	3.36	3.52	20.32	1.10	.23
1.03	.59	.58	1.20	1.60	5.84	2.40	.45
8.44	1.81	.07	1.87	4.71	6.64	6.25	.31
7.37	.06	.05	4.11	7.97	10.54	.05	.79
2.22	.32	.03	2.01	6.46	7.67	.21	1.95
2.52	.62	.16	.95	5.48	5.74	.31	1.06
2.14	.46	.19	1.18	5.95	7.76	.87	1.29
.58	.18	.01	4.47	3.35	13.67	.01	.70
1.73	.71	.16	2.25	1.90	7.37	.42	1.67
4.16	.13	.11	2.98	2.09	13.84	2.37	1.22
.87	.53	.33	3.06	7.33	8.44	.52	3.25
6.65	—	.22	1.12	4.10	11.31	.48	2.73
1.41	.26	.37	1.14	2.42	4.37	1.37	.66
.39	.54	.18	6.50	10.26	15.64	.33	1.75
.43	.10	.17	6.12	5.10	10.10	.26	1.10
.76	.46	.17	8.06	10.13	12.03	.18	.76
1.92	1.51	.16	1.38	1.98	4.01	.37	.29
.86	1.72	.21	1.48	2.95	15.19	.21	1.33
.19	1.96	.30	2.41	4.86	19.19	.02	1.26
.60	2.84	.08	.84	2.69	10.03	.10	4.06
1.10	.78	.19	1.43	2.38	16.65	.27	.65
.96	3.13	.28	1.37	3.12	11.68	.32	1.07
1.14	4.15	.27	1.15	2.91	11.31	.25	.81

CHAPTER 8

Key Business Ratios

DEFINITIONS—KEY RATIOS

HOW THE RATIOS ARE FIGURED

To the economist and the statistician, terms like "median" and "quartile" are everyday working language, no more mysterious than "gross markup" to the retail store proprietor. But though they involve precious dollars and cents, their precise meaning is foggy to many businessmen.

In the ratio table following, three figures appear under each ratio heading for each wholesale line. The center figure, in bold type, is the *median;* the figures immediately above and below the median are, respectively, the *upper* and *lower quartiles.* To understand their use, the executive must also know how they are calculated:

First, year-end financial statements from concerns covered by the survey are analyzed by Dun & Bradstreet statisticians, who calculate each ratio individually for each concern in the sample.

The individual ratio figures, entered on data-processing cards and segregated by line of business, are then arranged in order of magnitude—the best ratio figure at the top, the weakest at the bottom. The figure that falls just in the middle of this series becomes the *median* for that ratio in that line of business. The figure halfway between the median and the highest term of the series is the *upper quartile;* the term halfway between the median and the bottom of the series is the *lower quartile*.

In a strictly statistical sense, then, each median is the *typical ratio figure* for all the concerns studied in a given wholesale line. The upper and lower quartiles, in turn, typify the experience of the firms in the top half and the bottom half of the sample, respectively.

DEFINITIONS OF TERMS

COLLECTION PERIOD

The number of days that the total of trade accounts and notes receivable (including assigned accounts and discounted notes, if any), less reserves for bad debts, represents when compared with the annual net credit sales. Formula—divide the annual net credit sales by 365 days to obtain the average credit sales per day. Then divide the total of accounts and notes receivable (plus any discounted notes receivable) by the average credit sales per day to obtain the average collection period.

CURRENT ASSETS

Total of cash, accounts and notes receivable for the sale of merchandise in regular trade quarters, less any reserves for bad debts, advances on merchandise, inventory less any reserves, listed securities when not in excess of market, state and municipal bonds not in excess of market, and United States Government securities.

CURRENT DEBT

Total of all liabilities due within one year from statement date including current payments on serial notes, mortgages, debentures, or other funded debts. This item also includes current reserves such as gross reserves for Federal income and excess profit taxes, and reserves for contingencies set up for specific purposes, but does not include reserves for depreciation.

FIXED ASSETS

The sum of the cost value of land and the depreciated book values of buildings, leasehold improvements, fixtures, furniture, machinery, tools, and equipment.

FUNDED DEBT

Mortgages, bonds, debentures, gold notes, serial notes, or other obligations with maturity of more than one year from the statement date.

INVENTORY

The sum of raw material, material in process, and finished merchandise. It does not include supplies.

NET PROFITS

Profit after full depreciation on buildings, machinery, equipment, furniture, and other assets of a fixed nature; after reserves for Federal income and excess profit taxes; after reduction in the value of inventory to cost or market, whichever is lower; after charge-offs for bad debts; after miscellaneous reserves and adjustments; but before dividends or withdrawals.

NET SALES

The dollar volume of business transacted for 365 days net after deductions for returns, allowances, and discounts from gross sales.

NET SALES TO INVENTORY

The quotient obtained by dividing the annual net sales by the statement inventory. This quotient does not represent the actual physical turnover, which would be determined by reducing the annual net sales to the cost of goods sold and then dividing the resulting figure by the statement inventory.

NET WORKING CAPITAL

The excess of the current assets over the current debt.

TANGIBLE NET WORTH

The sum of all outstanding preferred or preference stocks (if any) and outstanding common stocks, surplus, and undivided profits, less any intangible items in the assets, such as goodwill, trademarks, patents, copyrights, leaseholds, mailing list, treasury stock, organization expenses, and underwriting discounts and expenses.

TURNOVER OF TANGIBLE NET WORTH

The quotient obtained by dividing annual net sales by tangible net worth.

TURNOVER OF NET WORKING CAPITAL

The quotient obtained by dividing annual net sales by net working capital.

KEY BUSINESS RATIOS—

Line of Business (and number of concerns reporting)	Current assets to current debt	Net profits on net sales	Net profits on tangible net worth	Net profits on net working capital	Net sales to tangible net worth
	Times	Per cent	Per cent	Per cent	Times
5511† Automobile Dealers (128)	2.73 1.90 1.53	1.95 1.29 0.76	16.47 10.69 6.07	21.39 15.37 9.26	12.99 8.38 5.39
5212 Building Materials (96)	4.44 2.49 1.67	3.57 1.81 0.70	11.84 7.36 2.29	18.67 11.53 3.19	5.22 3.45 2.47
5612 Clothing, Men's & Boys' (153)	4.51 2.51 1.84	4.42 2.63 1.49	15.38 8.82 3.76	15.44 9.71 4.55	4.45 3.14 2.21
5651 Clothing, Men's & Women's (75)	5.34 3.00 1.87	3.93 2.18 1.15	14.43 6.52 2.98	15.36 6.74 3.49	5.09 3.35 2.19
5311 Department Stores (202)	4.91 3.37 2.19	3.21 2.18 1.22	10.21 6.64 3.55	13.49 8.23 4.15	4.77 2.98 2.28
Discount Stores (180)	2.43 1.71 1.36	3.01 1.75 1.07	23.29 14.42 8.63	31.35 19.25 10.47	10.23 7.56 5.19
Discount Stores Leased Departments (36)	2.00 1.50 1.34	3.20 1.83 0.74	28.96 17.37 9.76	35.95 27.96 13.85	12.12 9.04 6.46
5392 Dry Goods (96)	5.20 3.03 1.90	4.24 2.67 0.88	13.89 6.55 2.57	17.93 6.87 3.01	5.06 3.01 1.78
5252 Farm Equipment (99)	2.65 1.76 1.43	3.27 1.79 1.07	17.07 9.38 4.36	20.59 10.95 4.71	7.26 5.05 3.22
5969 Farm & Garden Supplies (88)	5.90 2.72 1.75	5.47 2.62 0.95	17.42 8.24 3.08	31.82 15.54 6.07	4.53 2.96 1.99
5613 Furnishings, Men's (83)	5.83 3.35 2.02	4.55 1.87 0.91	12.37 6.76 2.93	18.81 9.06 3.19	4.07 2.75 2.01
5712 Furniture (175)	5.18 3.19 1.96	5.04 2.39 0.92	10.34 6.00 2.90	11.14 6.74 2.99	4.19 2.49 1.61
5541 Gasoline Service Stations (84)	3.73 2.22 1.55	6.05 2.35 0.76	18.70 8.59 2.62	34.89 18.78 5.79	5.35 3.29 2.06
5411 Groceries & Meats (156)	2.74 1.97 1.36	1.80 1.30 0.81	16.98 12.15 6.53	49.77 22.38 15.66	11.68 9.04 6.79

†SIC (Standard Industrial Classification) Categories

RETAILING

Net sales to net working capital	Collection period	Net sales to inventory	Fixed assets to tangible net worth	Current debt to tangible net worth	Total debt to tangible net worth	Inventory to net working capital	Current debt to inventory	Funded debts to net working capital
Times	Days	Times	Per cent	Per cent	Per cent	Per cent	Per cent	Per cent
17.10	*	11.3	11.8	50.0	101.7	92.4	67.3	2.8
12.09	*	8.8	20.9	87.5	138.5	137.4	83.7	25.7
7.82	*	7.1	40.4	138.2	198.9	205.5	96.0	54.2
9.81	42	15.1	11.9	21.8	60.6	42.6	58.4	13.0
5.36	52	7.7	24.8	45.5	89.7	60.7	116.8	37.0
3.41	78	5.2	48.4	88.0	143.9	85.2	181.7	66.6
5.22	*	5.0	6.4	26.5	74.8	69.6	40.5	12.0
3.73	*	3.7	12.2	59.8	116.6	97.7	68.1	28.6
2.72	*	2.8	26.1	110.0	197.6	140.7	97.4	55.2
5.53	*	6.3	4.2	23.9	61.3	50.7	35.0	26.5
3.70	*	4.4	13.1	47.0	91.7	95.8	67.0	39.7
2.47	*	3.2	30.0	100.4	201.2	121.8	117.3	71.8
5.71	*	7.3	9.7	19.8	43.6	60.1	39.4	18.3
4.08	*	5.4	24.9	32.9	69.4	76.6	64.7	33.7
2.86	*	3.9	47.9	61.0	103.9	99.5	90.7	57.4
15.73	*	7.5	14.1	60.0	93.3	105.2	61.5	16.6
10.07	*	5.8	27.6	104.5	153.5	166.0	79.9	38.0
5.91	*	4.4	55.9	179.6	270.2	207.8	107.2	93.3
19.64	*	8.4	12.9	79.4	105.2	136.2	56.7	12.1
12.81	*	6.1	29.3	152.0	168.9	192.5	86.7	33.3
7.15	*	4.7	45.0	209.7	264.8	294.9	107.3	49.2
6.48	*	6.2	7.0	21.7	45.2	58.2	33.1	11.0
3.52	*	4.1	16.1	42.2	82.0	95.8	62.5	26.8
2.24	*	2.9	37.3	84.3	180.4	145.3	93.6	75.6
9.54	17	5.6	9.7	49.1	72.5	101.4	62.3	9.7
5.82	28	3.3	16.4	107.8	139.9	152.6	82.9	27.7
4.30	42	2.6	34.1	203.2	237.6	236.7	101.5	50.7
8.32	*	14.7	15.4	16.3	34.1	36.2	44.9	13.6
5.26	*	9.3	33.2	32.0	62.9	55.6	79.3	30.4
3.04	*	5.8	62.7	68.8	108.9	89.9	210.8	64.9
5.54	*	5.0	3.8	20.7	73.8	77.0	28.6	8.8
3.40	*	3.5	11.0	37.3	124.5	108.9	43.1	27.3
2.34	*	2.4	32.7	78.0	169.3	146.2	74.8	79.8
4.83	51	6.2	4.1	22.8	56.7	31.7	54.9	11.9
2.52	110	4.8	9.9	44.5	97.2	56.1	88.8	24.3
1.67	199	3.6	25.6	90.2	210.9	103.0	137.3	48.4
9.51	*	21.2	27.5	18.0	37.4	42.4	66.4	17.0
6.76	*	11.0	49.8	31.1	68.6	64.4	113.6	47.7
4.41	*	5.4	78.3	79.1	124.9	114.6	228.5	101.2
37.32	*	23.0	35.8	31.5	60.2	80.0	64.8	32.8
20.21	*	16.6	59.7	46.8	87.1	118.4	88.7	66.1
13.00	*	12.7	86.8	73.0	156.4	177.1	124.9	143.5

KEY BUSINESS RATIOS—

Line of Business (and number of concerns reporting)	Current assets to current debt	Net profits on net sales	Net profits on tangible net worth	Net profits on net working capital	Net sales to tangible net worth
	Times	Per cent	Per cent	Per cent	Times
5251 Hardware (99)	7.02 / 3.62 / 2.01	3.88 / 2.16 / 0.74	9.77 / 5.49 / 1.98	13.77 / 7.17 / 2.66	3.12 / 2.36 / 1.55
5722 Household Appliances (106)	3.39 / 2.21 / 1.70	4.13 / 2.64 / 1.29	14.88 / 10.47 / 5.56	19.58 / 12.53 / 5.71	5.71 / 4.28 / 2.62
5641 Infants' & Children's Wear (50)	4.83 / 3.07 / 1.99	2.63 / 1.48 / 0.57	17.16 / 7.34 / 1.73	20.75 / 9.57 / 2.10	5.48 / 3.54 / 2.38
5971 Jewelers (63)	4.23 / 2.90 / 2.05	5.69 / 3.39 / 1.46	11.76 / 7.54 / 4.23	12.15 / 8.82 / 4.44	3.13 / 2.04 / 1.47
5211 Lumber Yards (140)	7.29 / 3.72 / 2.24	3.73 / 1.89 / 0.70	8.17 / 4.93 / 1.82	11.24 / 7.08 / 3.15	3.36 / 2.57 / 1.80
5231 Paint, Glass & Wallpaper (39)	8.63 / 4.57 / 2.63	3.89 / 2.03 / 0.44(L)	11.90 / 8.03 / 1.29(L)	21.44 / 10.20 / 2.51(L)	3.79 / 2.67 / 2.06
566 Shoes, Men's, Women's & Children's (112)	5.37 / 3.12 / 2.34	4.49 / 2.69 / 1.05	14.54 / 9.02 / 3.24	18.21 / 9.93 / 3.44	4.71 / 3.21 / 2.12
5531 Tires, Batteries & Accessories (69)	3.88 / 2.27 / 1.61	4.21 / 2.62 / 0.85	20.02 / 7.49 / 2.00	24.88 / 12.07 / 2.58	5.16 / 3.76 / 2.72
5331 Variety Stores (63)	4.85 / 3.58 / 2.75	4.31 / 2.16 / 1.16	11.81 / 8.37 / 3.33	19.39 / 9.87 / 4.64	4.40 / 3.08 / 2.28
5621 Women's Specialty Shops (208)	3.80 / 2.45 / 1.66	4.02 / 1.91 / 0.81	15.91 / 6.15 / 2.85	17.75 / 8.07 / 3.35	6.13 / 3.93 / 2.53

L (Loss)

RETAILING, Continued

Net sales to net working capital	Collection period	Net sales to inventory	Fixed assets to tangible net worth	Current debt to tangible net worth	Total debt to tangible net worth	Inventory to net working capital	Current debt to inventory	Funded debts to net working capital
Times	Days	Times	Per cent	Per cent	Per cent	Per cent	Per cent	Per cent
4.91	*	4.9	6.8	12.0	40.7	64.6	24.5	21.1
2.96	*	3.4	18.7	30.0	94.0	85.6	47.3	46.8
2.24	*	2.9	37.2	62.9	156.9	120.3	79.6	74.4
7.37	24	8.2	5.1	38.4	74.5	53.6	69.5	6.9
4.99	42	5.8	10.6	69.0	116.9	93.0	97.1	19.9
3.09	69	3.9	23.4	106.4	158.3	129.0	131.3	55.5
6.66	*	6.6	7.3	20.7	70.2	74.7	35.2	11.4
3.96	*	4.8	14.3	40.3	104.4	98.9	56.7	25.7
2.87	*	3.0	30.7	74.7	136.4	129.5	83.6	37.1
3.30	*	4.3	2.4	34.2	65.0	54.5	42.9	9.7
2.09	*	2.9	8.2	51.5	97.1	75.8	74.7	29.1
1.52	*	1.9	20.2	116.0	198.6	116.3	138.0	49.7
4.53	43	6.8	12.2	14.4	42.5	47.8	29.9	11.5
3.32	57	5.0	20.6	32.9	70.2	66.4	65.2	27.5
2.28	83	3.6	36.9	62.7	109.7	95.9	110.6	45.7
5.37	*	6.7	6.6	8.8	41.5	65.4	16.9	11.7
3.47	*	4.8	20.7	20.0	70.8	75.9	46.7	34.7
2.48	*	3.7	50.7	50.1	220.4	88.4	80.0	60.1
5.43	*	4.5	5.4	20.4	51.4	84.5	24.6	10.1
3.54	*	3.5	12.2	39.4	78.7	110.5	40.6	20.8
2.60	*	2.5	21.8	63.7	96.2	138.9	60.7	34.6
7.54	*	8.4	8.6	33.2	70.0	53.5	45.6	17.3
5.04	*	5.9	18.2	62.2	118.2	86.0	96.5	45.1
3.50	*	3.9	54.2	106.3	201.1	129.8	180.3	66.3
5.40	*	6.0	15.4	19.0	22.0	82.6	25.9	15.7
4.25	*	4.3	27.4	29.9	50.1	100.7	39.9	31.4
3.40	*	3.5	37.5	40.9	90.3	123.3	55.6	38.5
8.23	*	9.4	6.7	28.1	69.8	46.7	56.7	13.7
4.65	*	6.7	18.1	55.0	116.9	84.2	90.0	29.5
3.28	*	4.8	38.4	106.4	160.0	120.8	143.2	43.6

KEY BUSINESS RATIOS—

Line of Business (and number of concerns reporting)	Current assets to current debt	Net profits on net sales	Net profits on tangible net worth	Net profits on net working capital	Net sales to tangible net worth
	Times	Per cent	Per cent	Per cent	Times
5077*	3.97	3.63	13.53	15.88	6.85
Air Condtg. &	2.25	1.77	8.00	9.72	5.11
Refrigtn. Equipt. (47)	1.70	0.69	3.83	4.14	3.38
5035	3.01	2.02	13.61	16.12	8.82
Apparel and	2.06	1.07	7.41	8.14	5.77
Accessories (102)	1.68	0.65	2.66	3.45	3.86
5013	4.08	2.80	12.19	15.19	5.24
Automobile Parts	2.68	1.65	5.96	7.48	3.72
& Access. (218)	1.92	0.47	1.46	1.97	2.81
5029	3.78	3.60	19.71	27.77	7.67
Chemicals &	2.34	1.89	9.99	16.20	4.47
Allied Pdts. (55)	1.62	0.97	4.70	7.20	3.67
5094	2.46	0.88	12.19	15.68	23.80
Cigars, Cigs. &	1.90	0.41	6.71	9.27	14.40
Tobacco (89)	1.52	0.23	4.18	5.94	9.56
5082	3.19	3.20	16.22	20.76	7.38
Comml. & Industl.	2.34	1.94	9.55	11.25	4.80
Machy. & Equipt. (211)	1.73	1.01	4.51	4.78	3.19
5045	3.57	1.30	13.32	15.55	19.58
Confectionery (35)	2.60	0.66	7.96	9.39	10.53
	1.83	0.24	4.18	4.48	6.36
5043	2.63	1.87	13.17	34.10	9.81
Dairy Products (60)	1.71	1.23	8.59	19.57	6.72
	1.22	0.62	4.02	10.59	4.29
5022	3.17	2.79	16.85	19.41	9.11
Drugs & Drug	2.58	1.64	9.03	10.58	5.89
Sundries (110)	1.79	0.60	4.83	5.93	4.08
5032	3.12	1.85	10.74	11.89	10.53
Dry Goods (132)	1.92	0.91	4.99	5.33	6.10
	1.48	0.26	1.80	2.03	3.82
5062–63	2.93	3.18	15.12	18.89	8.12
Electrical Parts	2.06	1.94	9.52	10.99	5.52
& Supplies (156)	1.59	1.02	5.43	6.97	3.71
5065	3.78	3.31	13.69	15.71	6.10
Electronic Parts	2.56	2.34	9.79	9.86	4.25
& Equipt. (56)	1.86	1.59	5.67	5.90	2.77
5083	4.26	3.46	13.58	18.77	6.41
Farm Machinery &	2.53	1.54	7.32	10.84	4.68
Equipment (52)	1.89	0.42	2.99	3.29	3.16
5048	5.15	2.58	18.03	45.82	15.43
Fruits & Produce,	2.72	0.90	9.19	17.19	9.72
Fresh (60)	1.64	0.41	4.50	8.99	5.32
5097	3.46	3.53	15.32	19.09	8.16
Furniture & Home	2.06	1.93	8.77	10.41	5.17
Furnishings (65)	1.63	0.73	5.89	5.99	3.19

*SIC Categories

WHOLESALING

Net sales to net working capital	Collection period	Net sales to inventory	Fixed assets to tangible net worth	Current debt to tangible net worth	Total debt to tangible net worth	Inventory to net working capital	Current debt to inventory	Funded debts to net working capital
Times	Days	Times	Per cent	Per cent	Per cent	Per cent	Per cent	Per cent
7.71	35	10.1	6.1	28.6	51.9	53.1	48.8	12.6
5.98	43	7.0	8.9	69.3	83.1	78.0	83.8	22.1
3.57	53	4.6	30.4	113.6	142.6	128.6	143.7	33.2
10.07	26	10.6	2.2	47.1	64.9	56.4	64.0	6.4
6.39	42	6.3	6.4	82.3	144.8	85.9	106.4	28.1
4.21	69	5.0	21.9	121.5	196.2	120.5	142.7	59.2
6.49	29	6.3	7.2	26.6	58.5	73.6	45.1	11.7
4.61	35	4.6	15.1	50.0	90.8	96.9	64.5	28.5
3.42	43	3.5	28.5	86.1	143.4	126.2	91.6	49.1
9.80	32	16.2	10.0	27.0	50.2	35.4	84.6	21.6
6.09	39	10.6	21.4	54.0	111.5	66.6	122.3	37.0
4.11	49	7.3	46.0	96.0	150.1	91.2	202.9	63.8
29.66	12	28.2	7.0	53.5	87.4	75.2	79.2	10.1
17.73	15	20.6	15.6	91.0	108.9	99.8	112.0	19.5
13.77	21	14.3	30.2	147.0	191.2	137.0	170.0	35.0
9.17	31	10.9	6.8	37.0	74.4	56.4	58.9	6.7
5.97	39	6.8	13.6	61.3	112.0	80.4	92.8	22.4
4.07	53	5.0	32.0	109.3	177.7	111.1	146.0	42.5
21.25	8	22.8	5.2	31.1	46.1	79.6	45.2	14.3
10.81	15	11.9	13.7	60.5	134.7	98.7	67.4	24.8
8.50	23	9.0	31.5	120.2	193.0	116.5	107.4	48.0
19.87	17	63.0	28.7	28.6	61.3	20.2	147.5	8.0
14.34	24	35.6	55.9	52.7	70.8	49.3	305.6	43.3
10.68	32	22.1	83.7	89.0	109.7	75.2	492.6	115.5
10.99	20	10.2	6.6	40.5	67.1	69.7	57.6	13.5
6.56	34	6.7	14.8	55.3	106.3	94.8	82.3	28.0
4.78	46	5.6	31.8	107.9	200.7	123.6	104.3	47.8
11.44	24	9.6	2.3	41.6	93.0	69.7	65.9	10.4
6.92	42	6.4	5.1	97.0	141.4	105.4	98.3	26.1
4.26	59	4.3	11.0	188.0	224.6	170.8	141.5	43.9
10.72	38	10.2	5.1	43.8	82.5	59.4	74.4	8.7
6.30	44	7.9	12.4	76.2	115.1	84.6	118.4	19.9
4.53	58	5.6	22.5	136.4	198.6	119.0	149.8	39.0
7.45	32	5.6	5.3	33.8	79.4	82.3	48.4	12.5
4.79	40	4.1	9.8	66.7	105.2	106.3	68.0	32.2
2.85	48	3.3	24.0	99.4	152.3	136.2	91.7	44.0
7.24	29	9.1	4.9	26.4	48.0	47.1	52.7	5.8
5.61	42	6.1	11.0	51.3	80.6	76.7	89.5	20.4
4.05	57	4.6	32.9	99.6	126.1	115.5	109.6	42.3
25.97	10	86.6	16.1	14.3	49.7	14.0	74.8	11.5
14.70	15	50.5	29.9	37.9	73.8	44.7	143.3	34.6
10.31	22	15.1	61.8	68.4	105.4	82.5	302.7	54.8
9.04	28	11.1	4.8	33.9	95.4	54.9	64.5	8.7
5.40	50	6.6	7.9	82.7	135.8	83.4	102.3	17.8
3.71	68	4.7	20.8	149.6	176.6	137.8	146.1	27.8

KEY BUSINESS RATIOS—

Line of Business (and number of concerns reporting)	Current assets to current debt	Net profits on net sales	Net profits on tangible net worth	Net profits on net working capital	Net sales to tangible net worth
	Times	Per cent	Per cent	Per cent	Times
5042 Groceries (207)	3.34	1.06	11.83	16.84	19.21
	2.17	0.58	7.14	8.51	10.71
	1.57	0.30	3.40	3.72	6.68
5072 Hardware (216)	4.52	2.72	10.09	12.64	5.81
	2.98	1.44	5.06	6.67	3.35
	1.88	0.40	1.97	2.19	2.49
5064 Household Appls., Electrical (111)	3.01	2.09	12.84	17.08	7.84
	2.23	1.41	8.09	10.01	5.15
	1.75	0.93	4.95	5.26	3.70
5098 Lumber & Bldg. Materials (165)	3.87	2.85	12.16	18.22	7.22
	2.24	1.55	7.34	9.25	4.64
	1.58	0.56	2.72	4.03	2.98
5047 Meats & Meat Products (54)	3.85	1.85	14.73	31.35	18.85
	2.43	0.92	10.00	19.51	10.95
	1.51	0.36	6.24	9.57	7.30
5091 Metals and Minerals (68)	3.54	3.81	14.28	21.80	5.86
	2.25	2.39	10.03	13.91	4.15
	1.64	0.92	6.21	6.84	2.58
5028 Paints and Varnishes (44)	5.37	3.69	12.08	15.04	4.54
	3.16	3.13	7.54	8.30	3.20
	2.31	1.07	4.10	4.89	2.31
5096 Paper (157)	3.51	2.02	10.76	12.69	7.14
	2.30	1.14	6.26	7.71	5.08
	1.82	0.53	2.56	3.78	3.85
5092 Petroleum Products (75)	2.72	3.19	15.24	38.62	8.03
	2.00	1.95	8.56	18.97	4.82
	1.52	0.79	4.76	7.49	2.70
5074 Plbg. & Htg. Supplies (190)	4.26	2.99	11.17	13.21	5.65
	2.64	1.77	6.44	7.41	4.00
	2.03	0.75	3.60	4.18	2.83
5044 Poultry & Pltry. Products (45)	3.19	2.00	15.13	30.37	15.10
	1.99	0.80	9.42	16.87	10.17
	1.46	0.13	2.29	3.65	6.44
5093 Scrap & Waste Materials (49)	3.04	3.93	21.41	41.14	8.41
	2.19	2.53	12.92	19.65	5.09
	1.56	1.69	8.23	9.24	3.31
5039 Shoes (57)	2.79	2.21	15.36	15.86	6.26
	2.11	1.39	6.72	8.19	4.33
	1.66	0.63	2.45	3.17	3.18
5014 Tires & Tubes (35)	2.86	3.45	21.05	30.22	5.84
	1.85	2.52	9.85	14.16	4.16
	1.44	1.41	6.90	7.59	2.94
5095 Wines & Liquors (83)	4.66	1.82	12.42	17.65	11.87
	2.45	0.97	7.80	11.21	7.97
	1.60	0.24	2.64	3.35	5.48

WHOLESALING, Continued

Net sales to net working capital	Collec-tion period	Net sales to inventory	Fixed assets to tangible net worth	Current debt to tangible net worth	Total debt to tangible net worth	Inventory to net working capital	Current debt to inventory	Funded debts to net working capital
Times	Days	Times	Per cent	Per cent	Per cent	Per cent	Per cent	Per cent
22.84	8	16.3	8.5	37.5	82.4	83.8	51.9	14.3
13.19	14	10.9	21.0	76.3	150.8	117.6	74.1	37.8
7.48	23	8.1	46.6	135.5	230.8	173.7	109.1	71.1
6.69	31	6.1	4.9	24.9	48.2	72.2	40.0	5.3
4.27	41	4.6	12.3	44.9	68.8	91.0	61.9	18.5
3.05	54	3.2	23.5	82.7	139.6	124.2	89.6	33.3
9.15	35	10.6	2.9	39.2	62.2	60.9	69.0	7.2
7.41	45	7.0	8.5	69.9	125.2	85.6	108.5	20.3
4.40	62	4.8	21.2	114.3	188.1	112.1	147.8	38.2
10.50	34	11.6	9.2	24.5	62.8	55.2	54.9	11.0
6.10	47	7.3	19.7	60.5	118.6	83.5	104.3	32.5
4.15	63	5.1	41.5	117.3	178.9	114.5	161.7	70.6
30.28	14	56.5	11.6	27.8	44.7	27.1	102.1	12.1
21.27	19	37.3	23.5	55.9	96.8	51.5	179.3	37.2
11.30	25	20.6	56.3	119.0	289.3	95.2	326.9	88.3
8.02	34	11.4	9.7	28.9	57.5	56.8	55.6	11.7
5.52	42	5.6	23.1	56.8	108.5	86.6	91.3	32.0
3.54	56	4.1	39.0	112.4	204.4	121.4	152.9	52.4
6.61	33	7.0	7.5	19.4	29.4	54.6	43.1	7.4
3.74	46	5.3	11.5	34.8	95.5	71.1	65.5	16.8
2.71	63	4.0	28.3	67.8	222.1	89.8	108.0	94.7
9.26	30	9.7	4.6	33.8	61.9	62.3	55.9	9.2
5.78	37	6.8	12.5	61.5	97.7	81.2	84.9	24.6
4.61	47	5.5	24.8	102.6	151.6	109.6	126.3	40.4
16.76	21	41.1	32.3	24.2	50.7	30.0	116.4	21.8
9.68	35	21.7	55.1	41.9	100.2	58.2	193.5	53.8
6.04	52	13.0	82.7	76.1	199.3	81.4	416.2	173.8
6.77	34	7.5	5.8	25.3	59.1	61.7	46.9	8.7
4.74	46	5.6	12.1	48.3	88.4	78.7	71.3	20.4
3.29	63	4.1	22.0	82.5	158.4	107.1	111.5	48.2
25.65	12	84.8	8.2	28.4	39.3	32.4	103.6	2.5
15.88	18	41.2	29.3	42.5	68.5	51.3	164.3	53.3
12.42	31	15.8	53.1	108.0	128.6	85.2	358.1	132.9
14.36	22	21.0	11.8	30.5	61.4	37.2	66.8	24.7
9.95	31	10.7	28.5	48.8	96.3	82.0	127.8	48.4
4.98	38	7.8	55.4	89.8	153.7	133.8	263.3	84.5
6.86	30	7.4	1.5	50.4	79.2	50.7	72.6	7.2
4.88	60	4.6	3.7	87.0	109.7	88.8	104.1	15.0
3.71	88	3.8	12.2	135.6	170.0	129.4	164.9	28.4
10.15	43	9.0	12.8	42.9	69.7	69.8	79.9	13.7
5.22	52	5.0	26.0	91.4	154.3	105.8	112.7	32.0
3.60	72	3.9	42.1	141.5	210.0	132.5	199.6	86.4
17.82	10	19.2	5.8	21.8	42.7	55.8	52.3	8.2
10.19	24	9.1	16.9	55.1	154.7	91.1	79.2	46.4
7.03	35	6.5	39.1	128.0	235.5	147.0	122.6	77.2

KEY BUSINESS RATIOS—

Line of Business (and number of concerns reporting)	Current assets to current debt	Net profits on net sales	Net profits on tangible net worth	Net profits on net working capital	Net sales to tangible net worth
	Times	Per cent	Per cent	Per cent	Times
3522*	4.06	6.29	22.72	41.68	4.77
Agricultural Implements	2.35	3.97	14.30	21.01	3.09
& Machinery (66)	1.76	2.84	9.08	12.16	2.39
3722-23-29	2.87	6.48	25.69	33.77	4.37
Airplane Parts &	2.15	3.78	10.03	15.94	2.90
Accessories (56)	1.57	2.29	5.76	10.19	2.14
3714	3.68	5.63	17.30	31.55	4.04
Automobile Parts	2.52	4.55	14.07	21.06	3.05
& Accessories (84)	2.07	3.46	10.83	15.96	2.25
205	2.65	3.78	16.83	66.23	6.33
Bakers (69)	1.89	1.52	8.40	37.59	4.49
	1.21	0.64	4.88	20.18	3.02
2515	3.92	4.17	14.32	26.37	4.99
Bedsprings &	2.56	2.12	8.74	13.25	3.11
Mattresses (49)	1.93	0.84	3.15	4.88	2.04
2331	2.14	1.93	21.12	29.01	14.79
Blouses &	1.70	0.92	13.08	15.20	9.77
Waists (51)	1.37	0.26	2.68	3.91	7.66
3712-13	4.32	4.45	14.91	25.38	5.40
Bodies. Auto,	2.15	3.00	8.20	14.84	3.62
Bus & Truck (37)	1.63	1.44	4.55	6.42	2.53
345	3.95	6.41	18.58	36.62	3.79
Bolts, Screws,	2.48	4.43	14.15	26.06	2.55
Nuts & Nails (65)	1.71	3.49	9.53	17.50	1.93
273	3.67	10.75	22.52	30.16	2.70
Books, Publishing	2.97	7.36	14.74	21.73	2.12
& Printing (43)	2.05	4.40	8.98	12.85	1.71
2082	3.63	6.28	15.26	47.75	2.80
Breweries (33)	2.29	3.17	8.21	22.36	2.25
	1.78	1.70(L)	1.82(L)	9.77(L)	1.68
287	3.00	3.77	11.71	28.05	6.13
Chemicals,	1.80	1.34	4.36	9.01	3.37
Agricultural (34)	1.48	0.53	1.66	3.02	1.83
281	2.69	8.77	16.93	42.94	2.63
Chemicals,	2.09	6.08	11.39	25.55	2.02
Industrial (60)	1.42	3.92	7.90	14.16	1.51
236	2.61	1.54	12.69	16.64	11.95
Child. & Infants	1.73	1.11	7.12	8.28	7.93
Outerwear (63)	1.38	0.08	1.80	1.86	6.14
2311	2.68	2.54	12.54	16.15	7.13
Coats & Suits,	1.90	1.15	7.13	8.16	4.35
Men's & Boys' (131)	1.49	0.51	2.22	2.57	3.13

* SIC Categories.

MANUFACTURING and CONSTRUCTION

Net sales to net working capital	Collection period	Net sales to inventory	Fixed assets to tangible net worth	Current debt to tangible net worth	Total debt to tangible net worth	inventory to net working capital	Current debt to inventory	Funded debts to net working capital
Times	Days	Times	Per cent	Per cent	Per cent	Per cent	Per cent	Per cent
7.75	29	6.9	19.6	24.4	49.7	69.3	44.6	25.6
4.65	43	4.0	36.3	42.5	80.8	105.9	69.5	40.2
3.15	61	3.2	54.2	76.0	107.7	145.8	99.0	54.5
6.90	36	9.0	33.1	33.6	44.8	58.1	77.6	18.6
4.94	48	6.8	46.8	52.3	74.5	84.7	104.5	36.4
3.48	63	4.2	70.1	83.4	118.4	111.2	155.7	65.7
7.07	33	8.6	23.3	24.9	43.5	62.1	59.8	17.4
5.13	40	5.8	38.2	36.5	64.7	81.7	81.5	36.9
3.42	49	4.4	53.5	55.5	101.1	108.7	115.7	64.3
29.40	14	37.6	62.7	19.8	43.1	37.3	123.1	39.1
13.80	17	27.2	80.2	30.9	67.7	54.3	202.9	87.2
9.56	22	18.4	102.4	48.4	121.0	120.9	283.8	228 5
7.78	29	12.5	16.2	21.1	37.3	47.0	48.6	9.4
5.92	42	7.5	29.2	35.5	43.6	70.0	105.3	17.9
3.60	55	5.6	54.0	61.0	97.6	101.5	144.5	62.6
18.51	27	22.7	4.7	78.8	78.5	56.1	122.8	6.8
12.26	39	14.1	10.0	124.5	149.9	77.8	181.8	16.6
8.39	45	9.9	21.4	202.7	255.7	150.1	236.1	34.9
7.45	34	10.1	22.3	25.2	66.6	52.8	58.4	19.0
5.41	42	6.3	38.5	59.2	94.9	83.0	91.0	37.4
3.40	53	4.1	63.6	98.2	119.1	143.3	121.0	61.1
7.82	29	14.3	32.5	21.9	34.3	61.8	53.9	16.9
4.77	35	5.7	49.9	34.9	70.2	81.4	82.3	34.4
3.35	41	4.5	71.8	61.4	106.2	113.4	147.9	81.7
4.42	52	7.5	12.9	29.0	51.5	52.5	61.4	14.5
2.51	71	3.8	31.3	45.4	66.0	67.3	91.2	25.4
1.97	93	3.2	46.2	64.6	85.2	78.7	177.7	55.4
11.04	7	21.9	52.7	15.7	24.8	31.7	102.8	18.6
6.84	18	12.6	67.6	20.5	45.8	51.2	161.1	64.8
5.18	26	11.0	89.3	33.1	74.6	73.9	193.7	92.7
10.82	26	11.0	44.4	31.8	72.9	47.3	77.5	26.8
6.72	45	7.5	57.8	58.8	132.9	83.1	115.5	63.9
3.78	65	5.4	77.1	120.9	211.2	134.0	199.7	102.0
7.10	40	9.5	38.9	20.0	32.6	56.5	79.1	44.6
5.18	44	7.3	67.2	31.5	64.6	73.4	100.8	85.0
3.16	57	5.3	87.9	55.7	111.7	112.5	160.8	153.5
15.27	22	11.0	5.3	62.5	104.8	64.3	84.9	11.9
9.97	31	7.1	13.6	122.6	178.0	112.4	115.4	29.7
6.41	42	5.8	27.3	206.4	344.4	180.3	172.7	70.8
8.67	25	6.6	4.0	45.8	79.3	71.6	67.1	7.1
5.19	53	5.0	7.0	83.0	134.7	103.3	97.5	18.9
3.53	84	3.5	18.6	170.1	221.4	156.1	145.6	37.5

KEY BUSINESS RATIOS—

Line of Business (and number of concerns reporting)	Current assets to current debt	Net profits on net sales	Net profits on tangible net worth	Net profits on net working capital	Net sales to tangible net worth
	Times	Per cent	Per cent	Per cent	Times
2337 Coats & Suits, Women's (99)	2.87 1.85 1.49	2.54 1.27 0.58	21.50 10.55 4.68	25.61 12.53 4.87	11.33 7.87 5.13
366 Communication Equipment (66)	3.58 2.23 1.63	5.37 4.24 2.09	15.47 10.65 6.72	20.91 14.14 8.43	4.27 2.71 2.15
327 Concrete, Gypsum & Plaster Prod. (80)	3.49 2.35 1.66	6.81 4.06 2.77	14.92 9.12 6.55	38.03 23.55 13.56	3.10 2.35 1.65
207 Confectionery (48)	4.25 2.69 1.72	7.82 2.92 0.96	17.27 12.34 7.02	32.56 22.29 13.07	4.98 3.07 2.27
353 Construction Machinery (75)	3.98 2.58 1.76	7.05 4.41 3.28	18.17 13.58 8.83	29.74 19.16 11.63	4.31 2.83 2.00
1511 Contractors, Bldg. Constr. (159)	2.07 1.51 1.24	2.69 1.42 0.59	18.18 9.69 3.52	33.14 16.66 5.69	11.98 7.18 4.00
1731 Contractors, Electrical (104)	3.23 2.06 1.53	4.61 2.25 0.91	19.43 11.74 3.85	28.18 15.87 6.18	7.97 5.27 3.52
1621 Contractors, Heavy Constr. (92)	3.04 1.67 1.21	6.61 3.24 0.99	23.47 11.51 4.12	58.80 24.38 7.00	6.21 3.66 2.08
1711 Contractors, Plumbing Heating & Air Cond. (80)	2.46 1.83 1.37	3.09 1.71 0.82	19.32 9.04 4.38	21.10 12.30 5.73	9.68 5.78 4.14
284 Cosmetics, Perfumes & Toilet Prep. (43)	3.55 2.61 2.10	6.05 4.09 1.34	19.74 12.39 5.45	33.43 17.59 7.40	4.68 3.20 2.40
2211* Cotton Cloth Mills (45)	4.11 2.98 2.26	6.16 4.87 3.05	13.77 10.97 8.36	24.07 18.21 13.76	2.72 1.99 1.43
202 Dairy Products (122)	2.34 1.80 1.32	2.62 1.58 0.90	13.47 8.12 4.41	40.52 25.95 12.72	7.29 4.98 3.54
2335 Dresses: Silk, Rayon & Acetate (126)	2.08 1.58 1.35	2.23 0.79 0.27	21.45 10.44 3.24	25.32 13.80 4.15	17.16 10.07 5.61
283 Drugs (56)	4.17 2.94 1.98	9.57 5.93 2.97	20.49 12.47 4.14	45.08 23.74 6.65	3.33 2.14 1.63
364 Electrical Parts & Supplies (59)	3.87 2.77 1.76	6.72 3.87 2.57	21.40 13.91 8.67	31.67 18.89 11.22	4.73 3.11 2.47

*SIC Categories   **Building trades contractors have no inventories in the credit sense of the term. As a general

MANUFACTURING and CONSTRUCTION, Continued

Net sales to net working capital	Collection period	Net sales to inventory	Fixed assets to tangible net worth	Current debt to tangible net worth	Total debt to tangible net worth	inventory to net working capital	Current debt to Inventory	Funded debts to net working capital
Times	Days	Times	Per cent	Per cent	Per cent	Per cent	Per cent	Per cent
13.64	25	18.5	2.6	47.3	52.8	41.3	98.1	9.5
9.16	44	9.5	5.1	99.0	138.5	78.5	141.0	26.2
5.45	55	6.8	10.7	185.2	260.5	146.5	209.4	44.6
5.21	44	7.5	20.6	28.1	55.7	54.3	68.4	27.1
3.57	58	5.2	37.0	50.3	93.6	76.4	96.0	45.6
2.57	77	3.7	58.3	89.3	137.7	109.1	142.1	76.9
7.08	42	15.3	44.3	18.7	41.3	31.7	73.1	13.2
5.15	52	9.8	65.6	36.3	62.1	52.9	150.3	46.4
3.66	69	6.2	90.8	54.3	130.2	74.8	258.5	93.5
10.11	12	10.1	33.2	20.7	35.2	55.0	51.5	16.1
5.36	22	8.5	45.9	30.6	55.2	76.4	80.4	38.0
3.91	28	5.6	75.1	56.6	113.6	133.6	125.7	95.2
7.42	35	7.2	20.6	22.7	47.3	64.2	52.8	16.6
4.00	52	4.4	33.6	44.4	73.8	86.7	70.0	44.6
2.71	68	3.1	48.5	67.9	114.6	115.3	99.2	66.4
22.10	**	**	8.9	62.1	90.3	**	**	12.7
11.11	**	**	20.7	135.2	196.0	**	**	42.1
6.51	**	**	43.8	238.4	290.2	**	**	132.1
10.87	**	**	10.7	35.4	64.9	**	**	7.1
7.05	**	**	22.3	69.3	119.4	**	**	24.0
4.40	**	**	32.6	122.0	199.8	**	**	54.8
16.38	**	**	30.0	25.8	59.7	**	**	8.9
8.21	**	**	50.3	62.5	109.3	**	**	40.5
3.74	**	**	79.0	138.3	180.9	**	**	76.9
12.50	**	**	9.9	57.1	117.2	**	**	22.6
7.55	**	**	18.9	98.3	156.1	**	**	48.9
5.24	**	**	32.1	171.8	260.0	**	**	70.1
8.35	29	11.5	23.7	25.8	40.0	47.5	80.0	6.9
4.84	37	8.5	32.3	37.8	63.2	61.9	100.0	34.1
3.43	50	6.8	52.4	80.6	151.8	77.3	144.3	79.5
5.69	29	7.1	35.4	17.6	28.7	56.2	48.4	17.6
4.57	46	5.7	49.0	22.9	42.3	72.5	67.7	33.9
2.87	63	4.6	66.5	40.7	149.2	89.8	108.5	60.2
22.42	14	60.7	40.5	24.7	38.1	30.4	136.3	20.4
14.34	23	31.1	62.8	40.1	67.1	53.0	254.1	56.0
10.44	30	18.6	85.9	63.3	105.5	95.9	458.7	110.2
20.34	28	21.4	5.1	78.3	72.4	57.5	128.9	21.7
11.46	41	13.2	10.3	140.5	147.2	95.8	196.0	36.7
6.90	52	7.7	17.5	229.2	228.0	140.7	274.5	50.0
6.60	37	8.8	22.2	19.6	28.9	40.0	51.4	6.8
3.97	44	6.5	37.7	31.4	54.6	67.0	92.1	32.4
2.63	60	4.4	54.2	40.8	88.9	96.2	125.0	79.4
6.19	31	7.1	24.8	24.3	57.8	56.2	61.0	23.7
4.06	40	5.4	36.0	44.9	104.5	82.4	80.4	41.8
3.19	50	4.3	55.4	87.2	188.3	123.7	117.0	71.2

rule, they have no customary selling terms, each contract being a special job for which individual terms are arranged.

KEY BUSINESS RATIOS—

Line of Business (and number of concerns reporting)	Current assets to current debt	Net profits on net sales	Net profits on tangible net worth	Net profits on net working capital	Ner sales to tangible net worth
	Times	Per cent	Per cent	Per cent	Times
367 Electronic Components & Accessories (80)	3.01 2.42 1.78	5.76 4.13 2.12	19.85 12.80 8.98	25.45 15.95 10.68	4.22 3.46 2.31
332 Foundries, Iron & Steel (58)	2.92 2.24 1.72	5.90 4.23 3.61	18.09 13.36 9.18	48.77 24.68 18.02	4.15 3.13 2.08
336 Foundries, Nonferrous (44)	3.84 2.59 1.91	6.93 3.48 1.30	17.23 10.72 4.58	33.32 21.19 10.27	4.35 2.82 2.14
203 Fruits & Vegetables, Canners (57)	2.72 1.68 1.34	5.28 2.51 1.30	16.86 10.13 6.44	32.86 18.34 9.78	5.27 3.56 2.51
2511–12 Furniture (106)	4.18 2.62 1.72	5.08 2.73 1.45	16.08 11.74 5.80	28.90 17.15 9.04	4.78 3.25 2.35
2371 Fur Garments & Accessories (40)	2.62 1.89 1.47	1.54 0.75 0.41	10.21 4.93 3.02	11.30 5.09 3.16	9.58 6.11 4.61
356 General Industrial Machinery (79)	3.52 2.48 1.82	7.22 5.75 3.94	18.81 14.16 11.27	29.15 24.57 17.72	4.12 2.34 1.85
204 Grain Mill Products (62)	4.43 2.48 1.66	3.43 1.74 0.87	13.03 8.38 3.98	29.54 16.64 6.55	5.78 4.20 3.14
342 Hardware & Tools (104)	4.38 2.95 2.02	7.91 5.22 3.34	20.60 12.04 7.83	29.08 18.08 11.19	3.50 2.01 1.49
343 Heating Apparatus & Plumbing Fixtures (41)	4.16 2.55 1.61	5.43 3.58 0.45	18.31 11.34 3.72	22.44 15.35 5.18	4.62 3.46 2.24
2251–52 Hosiery (53)	4.01 2.42 1.91	4.26 2.58 0.28	9.85 6.38 1.53	18.18 11.65 2.85	3.59 2.39 1.54
363 Household Appliances (49)	4.00 2.67 1.93	5.86 3.77 1.98	19.39 10.70 5.65	28.40 14.30 7.21	3.64 2.91 2.20
362 Industrial Apparatus, Electrical (50)	3.76 2.62 1.71	6.98 4.44 3.33	19.87 14.43 7.81	39.55 23.08 10.80	4.00 2.71 2.18
331 Iron & Steel, Integrated Operators (57)	3.59 2.69 2.13	6.71 5.67 3.41	12.40 9.98 6.81	27.84 20.89 11.80	2.73 2.19 1.54
2421 Lumber (81)	3.91 2.47 1.67	7.66 3.89 1.73	14.47 9.97 4.84	36.46 19.68 7.73	3.87 2.55 1.37

MANUFACTURING and CONSTRUCTION, Continued

Net sales to net working capital	Collec-tion period	Net sales to Inventory	Fixed assets to tangible net worth	Current debt to tangible net worth	Total debt to tangible net worth	Inventory to net working capital	Current debt to Inventory	Funded debts to net working capital
Times	Days	Times	Per cent	Per cent	Per cent	Per cent	Per cent	Per cent
6.46	44	7.6	25.3	38.7	62.4	59 4	68.9	26.9
4.22	58	5.4	47.1	55.9	102.9	80.3	95.2	44.4
2.88	71	3.5	65.3	88.0	148.2	112.8	141.6	77.2
10.78	35	21.5	45.2	26.5	51.3	43.6	85.2	25.8
6.27	40	10.4	60.4	36.2	72.2	65.7	137.6	51.5
4.62	52	6.3	75.7	49.5	108.6	101.9	260.2	105.7
7.34	29	18.0	33.4	21.4	38.0	30.8	85.1	13.2
5.29	37	13.5	51.4	35.8	58.0	46.7	134.6	30.6
3.80	48	7.7	64.7	47.9	105.0	74.6	196.3	68.0
11.79	14	6.4	40.0	25.9	50.1	88.2	52.6	19.3
6.41	21	4.5	53.9	67.6	95.4	171.7	82.2	40.7
4.63	36	3.0	75.1	117.7	143.3	243.3	107.8	111.1
8.61	30	10.4	21.4	21.1	44.4	54.5	52.1	14.6
4.94	44	7.1	35.2	38.7	66.3	75.5	80.7	26.1
3.33	54	5.2	55.8	74.8	115.7	127.4	130.5	56.3
10.25	24	16.2	1.3	56.1	**	40.9	96.1	**
6.84	44	7.2	3.6	102.0	**	89.4	134.7	**
4.94	66	5.4	7.8	175.8	**	129.6	211.9	**
6.66	41	6.9	25.8	23.2	44.0	64.9	54.5	10.9
4.02	51	4.9	40.4	40.7	77.3	78.6	90.4	29.4
2.99	69	4.1	64.1	68.4	130.5	105.2	130.6	62.0
14.33	16	20.8	30.6	16.9	34.2	41.3	59.0	16.8
7.49	28	11.9	55.3	30.8	72.2	65.5	109.0	41.4
5.68	39	8.7	69.8	53.3	103.9	114.6	138.1	76.9
4.51	34	5.8	24.7	18.4	32.5	60.7	44.0	13.9
3.21	42	4.0	38.3	30.3	60.2	80.4	65.1	41.7
2.51	57	3.0	57.0	59.1	145.6	110.7	106.3	79.4
7.02	31	7.1	23.6	24.2	46.5	65.6	60.9	9.2
4.72	45	5.3	38.8	43.4	100.6	95.7	79.8	34.7
3.13	55	4.2	65.2	97.9	125.2	144.9	113.1	73.8
6.91	29	6.7	27.2	16.4	31.3	67.7	44.9	8.7
4.89	35	4.0	43.0	32.9	59.9	90.0	63.2	22.1
2.78	52	3.2	59.7	62.2	114.3	136.9	91.5	75.8
6.37	34	7.2	23.5	23.1	51.7	67.0	59.7	17.9
3.93	50	4.6	34.3	41.2	87.1	85.8	70.8	38.0
2.74	71	3.2	63.3	66.8	150.3	126.4	98.6	63.8
6.75	37	7.7	28.7	25.7	40.2	63.0	57.0	9.5
4.52	46	5.1	43.3	39.0	66.1	87.3	85.1	27.1
3.00	58	3.9	49.9	67.4	109.0	120.5	122.8	50.3
5.40	25	7.6	42.9	16.9	21.3	65.4	49.4	20.8
4.06	30	4.9	63.3	26.8	49.8	85.4	64.2	55.0
3.46	41	4.3	81.6	36.0	74.7	101.2	97.5	105.2
7.12	26	7.7	23.0	13.4	34.5	56.6	59.9	24.5
4.30	40	5.6	46.1	31.0	70.5	71.9	82.3	52.3
2.89	53	3.7	77.4	54.7	118.6	134.8	128.3	125.6

KEY BUSINESS RATIOS—

Line of Business (and number of concerns reporting)	Current assets to current debt	Net profits on net sales	Net profits on tangible net worth	Net profits on net working capital	Net sales to tangible net worth
	Times	Per cent	Per cent	Per cent	Times
359 Machine Shops (105)	3.30	6.91	23.86	50.55	4.12
	2.08	4.28	15.09	30.12	2.99
	1.58	2.39	8.00	18.67	2.11
2011 Meats & Provisions, Packers (101)	3.79	1.41	12.53	29.71	13.64
	2.56	0.83	8.52	15.71	8.62
	1.76	0.42	3.60	8.76	6.04
382 Mechanical Instruments (46)	3.62	8.39	19.86	39.87	3.47
	2.82	6.37	15.58	21.93	2.40
	1.83	4.75	11.36	16.61	1.89
384 Medical, Surgical & Dental Equipment (35)	4.87	8.58	18.13	37.17	3.52
	2.85	6.16	12.45	15.46	2.74
	1.83	2.52	6.40	7.55	1.93
3461* Metal Stampings (107)	3.19	6.18	19.87	50.56	4.74
	2.29	4.12	13.79	26.88	3.09
	1.65	2.85	7.77	14.83	2.00
354 Metalworking Machinery & Equipment (117)	3.45	7.86	18.61	40.93	3.57
	2.42	5.06	12.60	19.72	2.51
	1.74	3.02	7.91	12.88	1.79
2431 Millwork (40)	4.21	3.11	11.20	17.79	5.06
	2.71	1.96	5.21	10.87	3.55
	1.93	0.62	3.05	4.30	2.31
254 Office & Store Fixtures (48)	2.74	3.86	14.88	25.61	7.68
	1.98	1.26	6.88	14.56	4.32
	1.41	0.58	2.03	3.23	2.40
2253 Outerwear, Knitted (59)	2.53	3.43	20.13	34.70	10.19
	1.77	1.60	13.07	17.76	5.76
	1.40	1.01	5.65	10.32	4.20
2328 Overalls & Work Clothing (58)	4.71	3.81	13.91	17.93	5.01
	2.71	2.33	9.83	10.83	3.38
	1.74	1.07	6.91	7.07	2.63
2851 Paints, Varnishes & Lacquers (127)	5.47	5.59	17.26	25.97	3.89
	3.26	3.74	11.02	18.46	2.75
	2.38	1.67	5.63	9.13	2.08
2621 Paper (54)	3.62	7.20	10.93	38.77	2.70
	2.64	4.63	8.69	24.62	1.92
	1.87	1.70	5.35	15.80	1.41
265 Paper Boxes (67)	3.04	4.97	16.23	40.48	4.62
	2.22	3.33	10.44	19.21	3.43
	1.61	1.13	4.00	8.59	2.10
264 Paper Products, Converters (55)	4.09	5.87	15.13	26.98	4.61
	2.68	4.16	9.69	19.67	2.68
	1.88	1.82	6.09	9.86	2.05
2911 Petroleum Refining (54)	2.20	9.01	11.65	76.18	2.87
	1.43	5.31	8.60	35.75	1.37
	1.00	2.42	3.34	15.57	1.06

*SIC Categories

MANUFACTURING and CONSTRUCTION, Continued

Net sales to net working capital	Collection period	Net sales to inventory	Fixed assets to tangible net worth	Current debt to tangible net worth	Total debt to tangible net worth	Inventory to net working capital	Current debt to inventory	Funded debts to net working capital
Times	Days	Times	Per cent	Per cent	Per cent	Per cent	Per cent	Per cent
9.27	30	22.3	28.8	24.7	47.3	29.1	84.9	13.9
5.97	43	11.7	45.0	39.3	78.1	65.9	119.6	43.4
4.14	53	6.5	74.9	71.0	145.2	109.6	270.2	104.3
28.99	9	47.4	39.5	17.0	33.2	41.6	69.0	26.5
19.30	12	31.1	51.3	28.6	73.8	66.4	98.4	55.2
11.70	15	21.1	75.3	63.0	108.4	98.6	150.8	99.5
4.67	42	7.2	23.9	28.3	45.9	65.6	49.3	16.5
3.71	53	4.3	36.3	36.9	65.0	80.7	76.2	31.5
2.67	64	3.7	44.4	65.1	121.8	100.4	120.9	61.2
6.78	35	8.7	14.3	19.3	53.4	52.6	46.8	18.2
3.66	47	5.7	24.5	33.8	67.0	72.5	66.4	39.0
2.63	67	3.9	47.4	50.4	100.6	111.8	127.3	79.7
10.02	26	10.4	34.9	20.7	42.7	57.8	67.7	15.4
6.06	37	7.7	49.7	40.4	74.2	80.8	101.6	43.7
4.23	48	5.8	74.1	67.6	123.4	110.4	154.2	70.1
7.74	33	14.6	30.5	24.6	43.5	46.6	57.8	11.1
4.20	49	6.7	43.2	39.7	77.2	69.5	99.8	29.4
2.90	63	3.6	66.6	65.5	127.6	92.0	221.5	73.6
7.39	36	10.1	19.6	26.4	44.8	43.8	55.0	14.6
4.78	53	7.7	28.2	39.6	77.1	70.3	93.0	23.3
3.86	63	6.5	46.7	83.3	178.3	103.3	138.4	48.4
10.83	25	13.1	11.9	36.5	39.4	53.3	75.0	22.4
6.36	49	7.8	27.7	61.3	85.8	81.1	112.9	34.8
3.78	63	4.5	61.4	117.5	169.7	131.0	176.7	52.4
13.98	23	9.8	7.6	59.1	72.4	74.6	73.5	14.5
8.24	38	6.3	23.3	94.1	126.6	122.8	111.5	36.5
5.40	52	4.4	51.6	171.8	222.7	212.5	140.3	85.3
6.60	37	5.0	6.3	23.4	66.6	62.5	40.5	15.7
3.93	50	3.6	16.3	48.2	122.0	89.3	65.4	38.7
2.97	59	3.1	33.9	98.0	192.5	142.0	93.5	59.6
6.66	34	9.0	18.7	16.9	28.6	47.5	44.0	8.8
4.53	40	6.4	32.9	26.0	54.5	65.9	74.0	23.2
3.32	56	5.0	46.9	43.5	80.9	86.2	104.3	45.8
7.49	27	10.3	56.4	14.9	36.3	43.4	76.4	60.2
5.41	35	8.4	83.4	20.7	57.9	70.5	92.8	110.4
3.84	40	6.8	107.0	37.4	102.2	100.3	121.4	183.8
9.99	27	13.8	44.6	22.8	54.2	50.0	70.5	35.9
6.74	37	8.7	61.4	34.0	96.1	84.8	110.0	64.7
4.23	46	5.9	83.0	66.9	118.3	109.1	164.6	120.3
9.23	26	9.8	28.1	18.5	31.3	48.9	60.5	6.7
4.88	38	7.4	43.3	32.9	57.4	72.4	90.9	24.8
3.42	53	5.4	61.6	73.3	103.5	111.5	116.7	62.3
13.78	24	18.4	11.7	9.6	9.2	45.9	100.0	34.4
6.96	40	14.1	31.9	18.3	25.0	79.6	136.5	143.0
4.54	49	8.8	72.5	43.8	86.0	124.8	193.6	204.0

KEY BUSINESS RATIOS—

Line of Business (and number of concerns reporting)	Current assets to current debt	Net profits on net sales	Net profits on tangible net worth	Net profits on net working capital	Net sales to tangible net worth
	Times	Per cent	Per cent	Per cent	Times
282 Plastics Materials & Synthetics (40)	2.75 **2.07** 1.32	6.81 **3.74** 2.53	21.93 **11.08** 7.29	36.83 **21.91** 14.32	4.69 **3.24** 2.02
2751 Printers, Job (84)	2.76 **2.14** 1.64	6.15 **3.43** 1.55	17.72 **9.37** 4.47	43.53 **21.56** 9.28	3.96 **2.94** 2.07
3811 Scientific Instruments (30)	4.60 **2.90** 2.30	8.19 **4.40** 1.42	18.39 **9.84** 4.35	28.97 **12.11** 4.57	3.53 **2.81** 2.04
2321–22 Shirts, Underwear & Pajamas, Men's (57)	2.34 **1.76** 1.48	3.02 **1.89** 1.30	16.56 **12.25** 7.71	20.03 **13.28** 8.46	8.24 **5.64** 4.01
3141 Shoes (115)	3.47 **2.19** 1.56	4.67 **2.00** 1.03	17.32 **9.85** 4.88	21.71 **12.59** 5.01	6.89 **4.12** 2.64
2086 Soft Drinks, Bottlers (73)	3.05 **1.95** 1.28	8.55 **5.04** 2.44	19.92 **13.60** 8.25	71.95 **45.31** 21.39	3.70 **2.78** 1.99
355 Special Industry Machinery (71)	3.69 **2.85** 1.93	7.44 **5.61** 3.13	17.08 **12.20** 8.85	29.78 **19.33** 11.32	3.53 **2.35** 1.84
344 Structural Iron & Steel, Fabricators (115)	3.20 **2.17** 1.46	5.66 **3.44** 1.39	16.58 **10.54** 4.64	33.54 **15.08** 7.25	4.96 **3.32** 2.35
394 Toys & Sporting Goods (44)	2.94 **2.09** 1.60	4.41 **2.39** 0.55	13.28 **7.84** 2.47	17.51 **10.86** 3.13	5.02 **3.41** 2.78
361 Transmission & Distribution Equipment, Electrical (44)	3.08 **2.45** 1.93	6.47 **4.33** 2.24	18.74 **13.56** 6.56	28.55 **19.59** 9.06	3.80 **2.94** 2.30
2327 Trousers, Men's & Boys' (41)	3.34 **2.12** 1.61	2.62 **1.13** 0.31	8.85 **5.11** 1.27	9.39 **5.58** 1.28	6.06 **4.01** 2.98
2341 Underwear, Women's & Children's (51)	2.56 **1.76** 1.37	2.04· **0.93** 0.32	13.02 **6.17** 2.27	22.06 **8.92** 3.16	9.40 **6.20** 4.90

**Job printers carry only current supplies such as paper, ink, binding materials and lead for type-casting.

MANUFACTURING and CONSTRUCTION, Continued

Net sales to net working capital	Collection period	Net sales to inventory	Fixed assets to tangible net worth	Current debt to tangible net worth	Total debt to tangible net worth	Inventory to net working capital	Current debt to inventory	Funded debts to net working capital
Times	Days	Times	Per cent	Per cent	Per cent	Per cent	Per cent	Per cent
10.79	37	12.9	25.8	24.1	37.9	53.4	90.4	10.1
6.41	49	9.6	45.5	51.7	82.5	89.9	124.6	35.1
4.25	58	5.9	69.0	85.0	177.6	109.0	223.5	66.9
10.29	32	**	47.2	22.0	50.4	**	**	22.5
6.46	43	**	62.0	40.9	81.5	**	**	48.0
4.65	60	**	86.8	61.0	128.7	**	**	132.5
4.95	34	7.2	21.4	22.4	53.0	52.6	51.5	17.4
3.35	54	4.9	33.3	38.6	65.9	71.8	66.6	37.6
2.70	73	3.7	49.0	57.0	163.6	104.2	101.0	57.9
10.28	31	6.4	2.5	59.3	108.0	87.9	67.6	11.7
6.29	48	4.5	7.3	121.0	152.7	137.3	93.6	29.5
5.38	64	3.4	22.2	180.4	294.7	193.8	134.2	57.6
10.26	31	8.4	11.6	31.9	62.8	63.3	55.6	13.6
5.54	48	5.6	20.1	68.2	108.9	96.7	88.0	27.8
3.58	61	4.7	34.0	132.1	213.2	163.7	149.6	53.6
15.11	12	32.4	48.9	15.4	42.1	25.8	86.2	67.3
7.87	21	19.9	82.9	30.2	74.8	56.8	225.4	92.0
4.29	30	11.3	121.4	55.8	136.7	87.2	436.5	220.7
4.45	47	6.7	21.2	24.6	54.0	48.9	59.0	18.8
3.63	58	5.1	35.2	39.1	86.9	69.7	88.2	41.6
2.62	81	3.6	50.4	64.6	147.1	93.8	121.9	76.2
8.86	36	10.3	22.9	30.4	43.8	52.5	71.5	7.3
4.86	52	6.1	37.8	51.3	91.2	74.7	116.8	27.5
3.44	70	4.0	74.0	104.1	155.0	131.2	170.7	76.5
6.87	33	7.2	17.5	39.4	68.1	72.1	67.0	23.0
4.66	52	5.2	28.7	70.2	103.4	86.9	94.6	31.1
3.25	83	3.9	48.5	114.6	160.4	131.0	148.5	61.6
5.27	46	7.0	23.5	31.3	45.1	59.8	60.2	7.0
4.07	53	4.6	31.8	48.3	78.9	93.1	79.4	28.4
3.35	65	3.8	44.5	80.5	128.3	108.1	101.8	63.6
6.45	31	6.4	2.9	36.5	80.7	66.1	60.0	8.7
4.94	52	4.3	7.9	81.7	112.8	99.5	83.4	18.3
3.45	78	3.3	13.3	152.5	166.8	152.2	120.8	28.3
14.51	33	10.3	4.4	61.1	86.8	55.5	84.2	15.2
7.56	42	7.7	10.3	105.8	156.7	120.9	116.1	20.1
5.94	54	5.4	27.7	195.2	281.0	186.8	171.1	31.9

How To Calculate Mark-Up and Selling Price To Provide a Desired Gross Margin

One of the most difficult controls to maintain in business is the average selling price which allows a business to make its budgeted gross margin and net profit (if expenses are kept under control). Here are the simple calculations needed to figure mark-up and selling price for a desired gross margin in any concern handling a variety of merchandise. Different profits, gross margins, and mark-ups will be used depending on the item. That is why it is important, for the profitability of the whole enterprise, to consider average gross margin. If, for example, one slow-moving item is marked down, and there is no leeway for this in the budget, the average gross margin and hence final net profit will suffer. This same situation develops in the popular use of loss leaders. These may stimulate volume of sales but may not build percent of net profit unless carefully controlled. Usually budgets allow for mark-downs.

GROSS MARGIN, MARK-UP, SELLING PRICE

GROSS MARGIN %	MARK-UP %	GROSS MARGIN %	MARK-UP %
5.0	5.3	28.0	38.9
7.5	8.1	30.0	42.9
10.0	11.1	31.0	45.0
12.0	13.7	32.0	47.1
13.0	15.0	33.0	49.3
14.0	16.3	34.0	51.6
15.0	17.7	35.0	53.9
16.0	19.1	37.0	58.8
17.0	20.5	39.0	64.0
18.0	22.0	40.0	66.7
19.0	23.5	42.0	72.5
20.0	25.0	45.0	81.9
22.0	28.2	47.0	88.8
25.0	33.3	50.0	100.0

To determine the mark-up needed to obtain a gross margin not shown in the chart above, use this formula: Gross Margin ÷ Cost of Goods Sold = Mark-Up. (Note: Cost of Goods Sold is difference between 100% and per cent of Gross Margin.)

Example

$$\frac{\text{Gross Margin desired 29\%}}{\text{Cost of Goods Sold 71\%}} = 71 \overline{)\ 29.00}^{\ .41 \text{ or } 41\% \text{ Mark-Up}}$$

To determine the selling price for an item that will yield a specific gross margin:

(1) Divide the cost of the item by the percent of Cost of Goods Sold and move the decimal two places to the right. Remember Cost of Goods Sold percentage is obtainable by subtracting per cent of Gross Margin from 100%.

124

Example

Gross Margin desired is 20%. Item cost $2.00

Formula used is $2.00 ÷ 80% = Selling Price

Moving the decimal two places $ 2.50   Selling Price
     to the right gives us 80) $200.00

(2) OR, use this method: take from the chart above the Mark-Up that corresponds to the Gross Margin desired. Multiply Cost of Goods by the Mark-Up and add the result to Cost of Goods. Result is the Selling Price.

Example

Mark-Up of 25% is opposite	$2.00	$2.00	Cost of Goods
desired Gross Margin of 20%	×.25	+.50	Gross Margin
	$ .50	$2.50	Selling Price